ROME BEFORE ROME

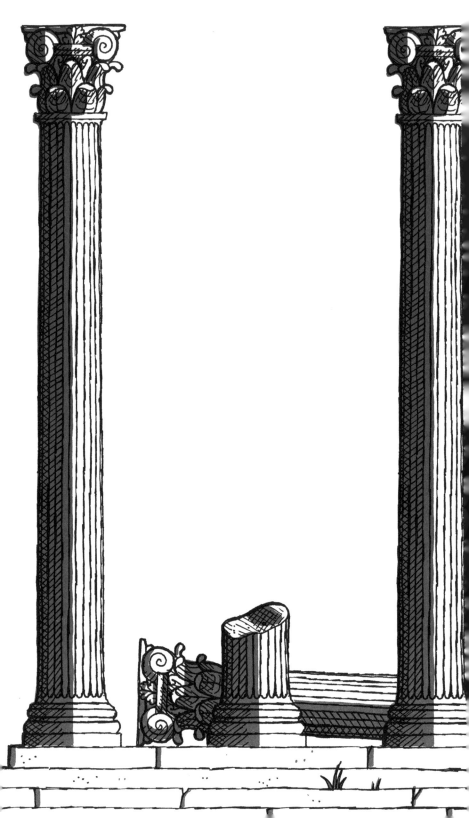

ROME BEFORE ROME

THE LEGENDS THAT SHAPED THE ROMANS

PHILIP MATYSZAK

WITH 41 ILLUSTRATIONS

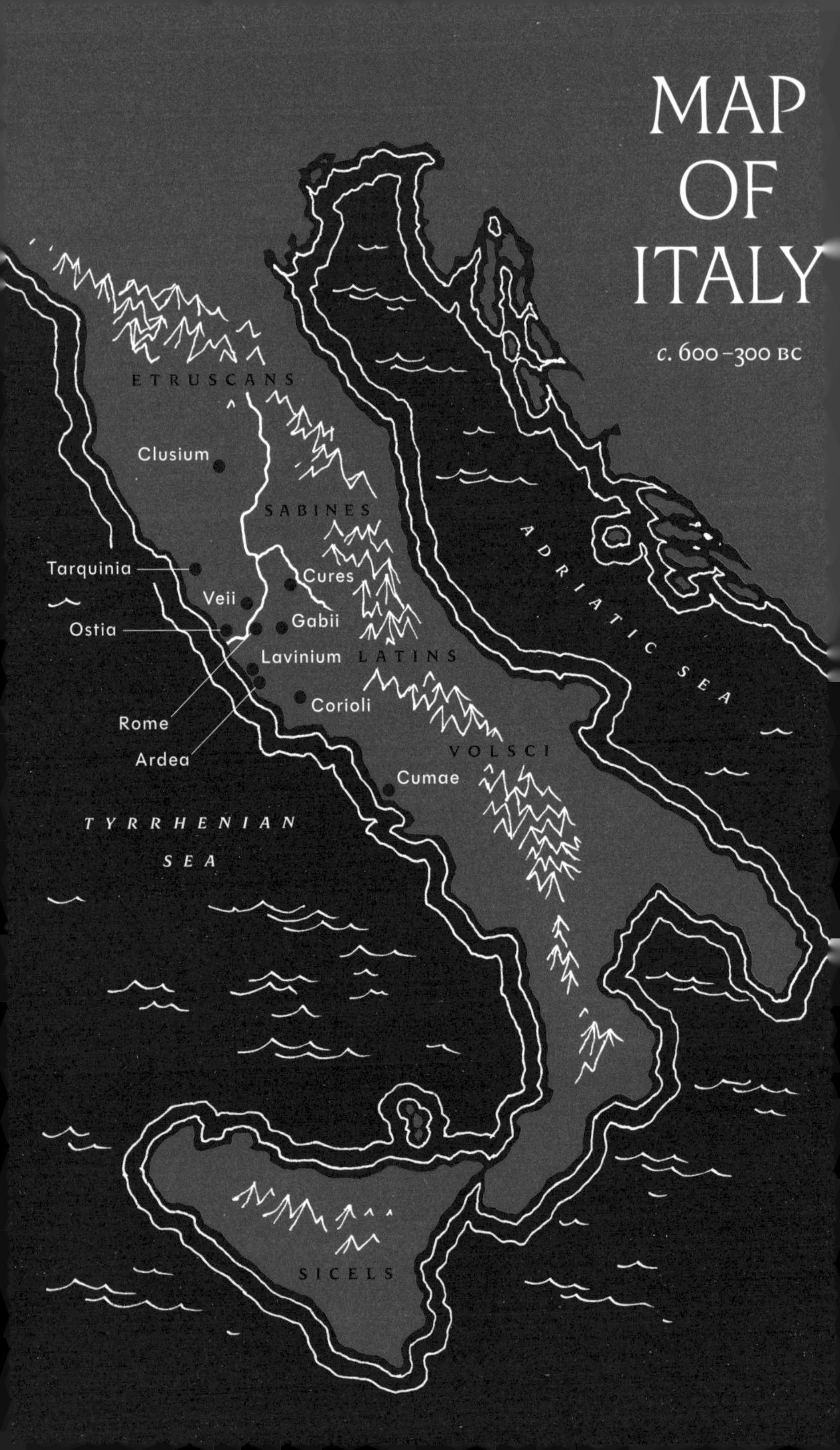

MAP
OF
ITALY

c. 600–300 BC

ETRUSCANS

Clusium

SABINES

Tarquinia

Veii

Cures

Ostia

Gabii

Lavinium

LATINS

Rome

Corioli

Ardea

VOLSCI

Cumae

TYRRHENIAN
SEA

ADRIATIC SEA

SICELS

CONTENTS

It is uncertain whether the task of recording the achievements of the Roman people from when they founded their city is worth the effort. Not only is the topic old, but it has been worked to death by a succession of new historians who think either that they are in possession of the 'real facts' or who believe that they can produce something better than the crude efforts of the ancients. Nevertheless, one reward for my labours will be that it takes my mind off the enduring troubles of the present day when I contemplate those brave days of old.

The tales that come from the time before the city was founded, or from when it was about to be founded, are more poetic legends than trustworthy, verifiable history. These will not be confirmed nor refuted here. It was the privilege of ancient writers to add dignity to tales of how their city was founded by adding a dash of the divine to human affairs. And if any people are allowed to sanctify their origins by attributing them to the divine, then their military glory has qualified the Romans.

Nevertheless, whatever one might think of these legends, I for one consider them less important than the main theme of this work. So I urge the reader to give much more attention to how people lived and what they believed ... and compare the discipline of that morality to how it is relaxed in the present day. We have plunged so low that today we can neither survive our vices nor endure their cure.

Also our subject is blanketed with obscurity. This is partly because of the passage of so much time, for just as things which are far away are so much harder to see, so time obscures events. It does not help that written records – the only trust-worthy descriptions of what happened – are few and far between. What little did once exist in priestly records and in public and private libraries has since gone up in smoke.

Again it is hard to choose one account over another or prefer one historian to the next. The true history has been falsified by noble families. They misappropriated heroic deeds of the past for themselves and wrongly claimed official titles in funeral orations and lying family genealogies. Because of this the record has been so muddled that there is no sure account of private lives or public events. Nor is there any contemporary writer whose work survives from those times, no one who actually experienced the events he describes and who would therefore constitute a dependable source.

Titus Livius (Livy)
Extracts from his epic work
From the Founding of the City, c. 21 BC

THE LEGENDS THAT MADE ROME

Romulus and Remus, wandering Aeneas, Horatius who held the bridge – were they real people or fantasies conjured up by later ages? Does it really matter whether Rome was founded as an inspired deed by two brothers or was simply a mundane village that rose to greatness?

Actually it does. One can learn a lot about a society from its legends – and every society has them, whether it is King Alfred burning the cakes or George Washington vandalizing cherry trees. The protagonists of these legends often embody the qualities which a society believes its best members once had, and which they should strive to have again. Likewise, the villains of these legends embody the anti-social qualities that society fears most. In short, legends are not just semi-fictional yarns from days of yore – they are the stories that tell a people who they are, what they should be and what they should fear.

Legends differ from myths and folklore in that they focus on humans in a historical setting. That historical setting is one which is generally accepted as being real. Though the humans may sometimes interact with gods or magical beings, even in such cases the point of the interaction is to bring out the innate qualities by which the human protagonist inspires others in his culture. That's basically what legends are for.

So, for example, the Swiss William Tell steadfastly shoots an apple off his child's head and later leads a revolution against the foreign occupiers of his land. England's Robin Hood takes from the rich, gives to the poor and courts the beautiful but independent Maid Marian. In Rome, Lucius Brutus over-throws a proud and vicious king and later executes his own sons for treason. Each of these legends tells something about the people among whom they arose.

The legends of Rome are important for two reasons. The first is that the Romans strongly identified with these stories. The very real clan of the Domitii Ahenobarbi took their name ('bronze-beards') from an episode in which a deity turned their ancestor's beard to bronze as his guarantee of victory in battle. The first of the ancient family of the Mucii Scaevolae ('the left-handed') got his name because he voluntarily thrust his right hand into a fire to prove that torturing him would be inef-fective. Julius Caesar partly based his right to be the first man in Rome upon his descent from Iulus, son of the Trojan hero Aeneas and the grandchild of a goddess. In turn Marcus Brutus assassinated Julius Caesar in 44 BC because his own legendary ancestor had freed Rome from the tyrannical King Tarquin and he felt obliged to do the same to the 'tyrant' Caesar. In Rome, as elsewhere, legends mattered.

The legends of early Rome were so important to the Romans, that they continue to have importance for us today. Not only can we not understand the Romans without understand-ing their legends, but we cannot understand Western culture either. Modern Europe did not only inherit the Latin language, along with Roman law and architecture: the continent is also heir to the legends of Rome. Furthermore, European culture has passed these legends on to the United States. That is why, for example, we have Troy in New York state. Roman legend is the origin of the phrase 'tall poppy syndrome', the custom of carrying brides across the threshold, and much else besides.

Because these legends are so fundamental to Western culture most people know at least some of them, and reference others without realizing that they do so. (For example, someone who is 'vindicated' is freed from the stigma of an unjust accusation – as was the legendary Vindicius.) However, few know of how these legends fit together, and indeed fit so coherently that the early history of Rome might be best described as a concatenation of legends.

These legends told the Romans that they were brave, chaste and honourable, respectful to their gods and beloved by them. They were victorious in battle, and on the few occasions that they failed militarily, they faced their fate unflinchingly. These standards the legions of Rome carried into battle just as they carried their iconic eagles, and often the Romans prevailed entirely through their unwavering belief in the inevitability of their victory.

This book examines the legends that made Rome, from when the first ancestor of the Romans fled from burning Troy, until history and legend merge almost a thousand years later. In between we shall discover how the river Tiber got its name and why criminals were tossed from the Tarpeian Rock. We shall also meet scheming villains and barbaric warlords – one of whom reckoned he was literally worth his weight in gold.

Not all of these tales make for comfortable reading. Roman attitudes were often very much at odds with what is acceptable today. Violence, rape and casual cruelty feature prominently in several tales, and our indignation is often directed not only at the deed but at how the Romans regarded it. Yet we cannot understand ancient Rome if we bowdlerize these stories to fit modern sensibilities and pretend such attitudes did not exist. Like Roman history, Roman legends are not for the squeamish. The Romans were a violent people living in violent times and their legends both reflect and (to later Romans) justify this.

Some of these legends may have a basis in fact – that Romulus and Remus were raised by a she-wolf becomes more credible when we learn that the word for a she-wolf, *lupa*, was also applied to a prostitute. Other Roman legends clearly have parallels in tales from Greece, Mesopotamia and Etruria, and these tell us much about the Mediterranean-wide exchange of ideas at the time.

All of the above are good reasons for discovering the legends of ancient Rome. Yet there is another reason just as relevant – most of them are cracking good stories in their own right and can be appreciated from a modern armchair as much as they were enjoyed around a campfire thousands of years ago.

I

BEFORE THE BEGINNING

They call Rome 'the Eternal City' and there is some justice in the name. The city – and its predecessors – go back a very long way. Well before the first Romans appeared on the Palatine, human settlement on that hill already had a long and complicated history. Both Roman legend and modern archaeology agree that there were people living in the locality generations before Romulus and Remus got around to founding their city. This is unsurprising, because even in prehistoric times the seven hills constituted prime real estate irresistible to settlers.

Legend tells that the very first settlers found the land in a literally chaotic state, for the ruler was Chaos – that primordial deity whom the Romans believed eventually settled down to become the god Janus, for whom the modern month of January is named. In the work of the poet Ovid, Janus claims:

> I dwelt on that land on the left bank of the Tiber's
>   shining waves.
> Where Rome is now, there stood an empty green forest,
>   and the mighty city was but pasture for a few cattle.
> My castle stood on the hill which the present age has
>   named the Janiculum after my name.
> I reigned in those days when gods walked the earth
>   and moved freely in the dwellings of mankind.
>
> (*Fasti* 1.241ff)

The castle of Janus was thus by some distance the oldest building in Rome – and was indeed by this legend one of the oldest structures in the world. This building still stood in Ovid's time, albeit in a considerably dilapidated condition, with a sacred grove alongside. In Ovid's poem Janus goes on to tell how he accommodated Saturn when that god fell out with Jupiter, and how Saturn taught agriculture to the local people. Saturn married and conceived a son called Picus, who made the mistake of spurning the witch-goddess Circe; she turned him into a woodpecker (the genus is still called *Picus* today). The grandson of Saturn had better luck, becoming the demigod Faunus, who later Romans associated with goat-footed Pan.

This first legend aside, the proto-Romans of 'Janus' definitely existed, and archaeologists have found the artefacts they left on the Palatine hill – over two thousand years before 753 BC (the traditional date for the founding of Rome). The identity of these early subjects of Janus remains mysterious. Roman legend calls them the Sicels.

'Whether the place was unoccupied or another people occupied the location before them [the Sicels] no one can now say', comments the writer Dionysius of Halicarnassus (*Roman Antiquities* 1.9). This statement still holds true some two thousand years after Dionysius wrote it. Aristotle adds that it was a Sicel king called Italus who gave his name to the entire peninsula: 'Communal meals appear to be an ancient institution. Those in Crete began with King Minos, while the tradition in Italy is much older. Historians reckon one of the settlers there, called Italus, became king ... and from him the people took the name of Italians' (*Politics* 7.1329b).

In the brutal world of prehistoric Italy those who occupied prime real estate such as the seven hills beside the Tiber had to fight to keep it. The Sicels were unable to do so, and some time around 1300 BC they were driven out of central Italy, eventually to settle down in Sicily – the island that still bears their name.

The Sicels were allegedly expelled by a marauding tribe from the mountains of central Italy, a people who called themselves the Pelasgians. These Pelasgians were eager to eradicate the memory of the Sicels and came to insist that they were in fact the original inhabitants of the region. To support this claim they took the name 'Aborigines' which means just that – 'The Originals'. At least so says Roman legend in a variety of texts including the *Origines* of Cato the Elder, one of Rome's first historians. (Cato's history is now lost, but it was referenced by several later historians including Polybius and Livy.)

When discussing the first peoples of Rome, modern ethnographers and archaeologists agree with Cato and his Roman colleagues up to a point (after which they disagree vehemently). Everyone agrees that the end of the Bronze Age (around 1200 BC) was a period of violent disruption and chaos, which involved the large-scale migrations of peoples around the Mediterranean world and beyond.

It also seems to be the case that at this time hill peoples from central Italy moved to the western coast and occupied – among other places – the territory around Rome. Beyond this broad outline of events modern research still finds the situation impenetrably murky, but the tellers of legend had much less difficulty explaining the issue to the Romans of their day. According to these legendeers, the first Romans were actually Greeks and Trojans.

THE GREEK CONNECTION

The storytellers of the Roman Republic were keen to link the prehistory of Rome with the legends and myths of ancient Greece. The peoples of early Italy shared much of their culture with the ancient Greeks, but it was painfully obvious that the Greeks had a much larger share of that culture than the Italians had. The Romans were keenly aware of their city's destiny to become the greatest power in the known world (even if much of that awareness came to them retrospectively after greatness had been achieved). Therefore, they wanted to make it clear that from the beginning – no, even before the beginning – Rome had its origins in the civilized Greek east. Rome's great destiny was in part because Rome's settlers were very different from the uncultured and barbarous hill tribes who founded the cities around them.

So before Rome was called Rome, before Italy was called Italy and before the Latins were called Latins, Roman legend tells us there was a city on the Palatine hill. In fact, the hill takes its name from that now-vanished city, which was a Greek – not Italiot – settlement called Pallantium. (Italiots were Greeks already settled elsewhere in Italy, for example in Capua.) This city was founded just before the outbreak of the Trojan War by a son of the Greek god Hermes, one Evander of Arcadia, who had displaced the Aborigines from the area of the seven hills just as the Aborigines had originally displaced the Sicels.

Why exactly Evander decided to abandon his native Greece and settle in Italy has never been explained, but it is true that around this time the Greeks were busily founding colonies everywhere from Emporion in Spain to Phanagoria in the Crimea. So many Greek colonies were established in southern Italy and Sicily that the region became known as Magna Graecia ('larger Greece'). It is no great stretch of the imagination, therefore, to conceive of Greek colonists sailing up the Tiber and forcing the locals off the seven hills.

I shall briefly explain ... the Arcadians have decided
  to live on this coast [of Italy]
They are descended from Pallas, these followers of the
  standard of King Evander
They have located their city in the hills and named
  it Pallantium.

(VERGIL, Aeneid 8.50ff)

Vergil: The Master Legendeer

The history of Rome before Rome is largely the creation of
one man, Publius Vergilius Maro. Yet the man who single-
handedly forged Rome's origin story was not from the city.
He was born in around 70 BC near what is today Mantua
and he was educated at Cremona in northern Italy. Since
this area was at the time part of the province of Cisalpine
Gaul, it can be argued that the greatest of Rome's poets was
not originally an Italian, let alone a Roman.

Vergil's life of peaceful scholarship was turned upside
down when Julius Caesar crossed the Rubicon in 49 BC and
plunged the Roman world into a catastrophic bout of civil
wars. Vergil's family lost their farm during the upheaval, and
Vergil's first work – the *Eclogues* – tells of a longing for the
(heavily idealized) rural life from which his family had been
so rudely ejected. This was followed by another set of poetic
rural raptures called the *Georgics*. The latter attracted the
attention of Rome's new ruler – the emperor Augustus.

Augustus was working hard to define a future direction
for Rome, and he well knew that one vital step in that

process was also to define Rome's past. Vergil got the job of doing this in his epic poem the *Aeneid*. Writing this account of how the hero Aeneas left Troy and (eventually) founded the city of Rome took the rest of Vergil's life, with Augustus regularly badgering him for updates. On his death Vergil is said to have wanted the entire thing burned – something Augustus clearly was not going to permit.

The epic survives to this day. It is at once the leading work of Latin literature, a shameless piece of pro-Augustan propaganda, and the text that defined how the ancient Romans saw their early history.

HERCULES IN 'ROME'

We hear more of the Greek colony of Pallantium because Vergil noted that Hercules had passed through Italy while returning from his tenth Labour. In his epic poem the *Aeneid* Vergil adroitly kidnaps Hercules for his own purposes, briefly diverting the hero to add a Greek dimension to one of the earliest legends of Rome.

The tenth Labour of Hercules involved taking the cattle of an inoffensive supernatural being called Geryon (killing the unfortunate individual in the process) and returning with his booty to Greece. While passing the site of Pallantium, Hercules encountered an uncouth and murderous thief called Cacus who stole some of the hero's cattle. We shall pass over the fact that, in taking the cattle from Geryon, Hercules could also have been described as an uncouth and murderous cattle thief, because Hercules was a hero, and just being heroic, Cacus was not. So everyone rejoiced when the righteously indignant

Hercules tracked down his stolen booty and messily disposed of Cacus in the process.

In commemoration of the deed the local people erected a temple to Hercules Victor. This they built at the foot of the Palatine hill in the contemporary style, the fashionable temple of those days being a circle of log pillars with a thatched roof.

At least so goes the legend. An ancient Roman might have argued that the truth of the story is proven by the fact that the Temple of Hercules Victor was still standing in the classical era. Indeed, that temple still stands today, located in a piazza by the river Tiber in what is now the centre of Rome. The design is definitely not that of a standard Greco-Roman temple (which is basically a box with a fancy frontage called a *pronaos*). However, while the original Temple of Hercules may indeed be even older than Rome, the current version is not, as it was rebuilt in marble during the second century BC.

In the generation of the Heroic Age after Hercules, the legends of Rome's foundation become inextricably entangled with the myths of ancient Greece. The decisive events were the Trojan War fought in the Dardanelles and the literally epic fallout from that distant war. So many stories were spun about the return of the Greek army from Troy that these tales became a particular subgenre of myth. The ancient storytellers scattered legendary heroes of the Trojan War across the Mediterranean world, and the Romans were not the only people to seize upon a wandering hero to buff up their home city's origin story.

The wandering hero selected by the Romans was Aeneas, for the interesting reason that he was not Greek. In the previous hundred years, before the poet Vergil informed the world

of the role of Aeneas in Rome's foundation, the Romans had fought a series of wars in Greece (the Macedonian Wars of 214–158 BC). Rome could already claim a Greek inheritance thanks to Evander, but making Rome's origins too Greek might kill the appeal of the *Aeneid*. Their wars in Greece had given the Romans a low opinion of their Mediterranean neighbours. Also there was the matter of the hugely disruptive Roman civil wars of recent decades, which everyone in the Augustan era was trying hard to forget. So the idea that a 'Greek' Rome had spent the past century fighting fellow Greeks would alienate a public very tired of civil wars of any kind and not that eager to identify with the Greeks in the first place.

Yet the connection with the mythical past and the cultural appeal of Greece could not be resisted. Homer's *Iliad* was almost as well known in Rome as in Greece, and the Romans were eager to write themselves into the legend. Perhaps, though, it would be politic for Rome to claim ancestry from the Trojan side of the legend. Which brings us to Aeneas the Trojan.

INTRODUCING AENEAS

Aeneas is considered the legendary ancestor of the Roman people, and as will be seen, he was also partly responsible for the promotion of Julius Caesar to divine status around a thousand years later. Aeneas fought on the Trojan side in the Trojan War and is often referred to by Roman poets as 'Trojan Aeneas', but he was not, in fact, originally from Troy. (A nice touch by the Roman poet Vergil, who was not, in fact, originally from Rome.)

The legend of the origins of Aeneas can be picked up at the point where Hercules finished his rampage through Italy and turned his attention to Troy. For reasons we need not go into here (all the Greco-Roman myths are entangled), Hercules killed off most of the Trojan royal family. The surviving male, Priam, took over the city. His aunt Themiste also survived the massacre because she had already left Troy to marry a nearby king elsewhere in the Troad (as the region around Troy was known). At the time that Hercules was severely diminishing the size of her family, Themiste increased it by giving birth to a son called Anchises.

While still a young man, Anchises was seduced by a beautiful woman whom he met on the slopes of Mount Ida near Troy. This casual liaison, as such liaisons are sometimes wont to do, had far-reaching consequences. In this case, the beautiful woman returned to Anchises several months later to inform him that he was now a father. Furthermore, she revealed that she was none other than the goddess Venus (Aphrodite to the Greeks) herself. The purpose of this return visit was to inform Anchises that she had awarded him custody of the child.

The baby was duly handed over. Venus had already given a name to the infant, explaining, 'His name will be Aeneas since I was overwhelmed with terrible grief (*ainion achos*) that I had sex with a mortal man' (*Homeric Hymn to Aphrodite* 198). Venus hastened to explain that Anchises should not take this grief personally. It was just that the immortal goddess was now doomed to see her lover and son age and die, while she remained eternally young.

This child was thus, technically speaking, Aeneas the Troadian, rather than Aeneas the Trojan. Following the instructions of Venus, he was raised by nymphs until manhood after which Anchises took him to Troy. There, as relatives of the now aged King Priam, the pair were made welcome as members of the royal household.

When the Trojan War began Aeneas naturally took the Trojan side, though Priam was somewhat reluctant to get him involved in the fighting. The king need not have worried, though, because his divine mother kept a vigilant eye on his safety. When Aeneas was badly wounded Venus plunged into the fray and rescued him, even though she herself was wounded in the fight (as Homer tells in the *Iliad* book 5).

Later, Aeneas had the rare distinction of facing the mighty Achilles in battle and surviving the experience. Admittedly he was saved from certain death only through the intervention of the god Poseidon. The sea-god usually favoured the Greeks, but he explained that he was prepared to make an exception for Aeneas because, 'He is destined to survive, so that his race might also survive ... The Son of Cronos [Zeus] has come to hate Priam's line, but mighty Aeneas will be a Trojan king, as shall his descendants in time to come' (*Iliad* 20.306ff).

In the *Iliad* Poseidon never explains what he meant by this cryptic utterance. However, these lines in a poem – already a thousand years old in Vergil's time – gave the poet a perfect hook with which to link the continuing story of Aeneas with the distant, mythical past. The Romans were thus able to consider themselves as 'Trojans', by the authority of Poseidon and the venerable *Iliad*.

Aeneas himself tells the tale of how he escaped from burning Troy in the second book of the *Aeneid*. After first fighting in the desperate chaos of the fallen city, he was persuaded by his mother Venus to gather the rest of his family and flee:

I

I bowed my neck and over my wide shoulders I laid the
    skin of a tawny lion and bent to lift the burden [of
    my father Anchises.]
[My son] little Iulus puts his hand in mine, and follows
    his father with halting steps,
With my wife following, we keep to the shadows; for I,
    who braved without thinking showers of missiles and
    the Greeks in battle array,
Am now alarmed by every breath of wind and startled
    by every sound, trembling with fear for my companion
    and my burden.

(VERGIL, *Aeneid* 2.721ff)

A NEW HOME

So began the epic journey of Aeneas from Troy to Italy. While
still in the streets of Troy he and his wife were separated in the
tumult, and he never saw her again. His father Anchises took
part in most of Aeneas's early adventures but died in Sicily
(Aeneas gave him a magnificent funeral), so of the original
family only Aeneas and his son Iulus came to see Italy.

The trip – as might be expected of a star-crossed hero – was
far from smooth. Aeneas detoured via newly founded Carthage
and dallied with the city's Queen Dido, and immediately on
reaching Italy he took a tour through the kingdom of Hades
with his newly deceased father as his guide. The purpose of this
visit was so that Vergil could move his hero beyond the Trojan
era to foresee the Rome of Augustus.

See now, the grandeur that awaits the Trojan race,
To whom fate will add children of Italian stock.

Magnificent spirits here wait to be born, in time
   to inherit our name.
Of all this I shall tell you as I reveal your destiny.
...

Glorious, the Empire of Rome shall extend to the
   ends of the earth, and its ambitions will reach
   for the heavens.
Seven hills shall that single city's wall enclose, and
   a race of heroes within.

   (*Aeneid* 6.756ff and 6.781ff)

The *Iliad* and the *Aeneid*

While one of these epic poems is written as a sequel to
the other and both contain many of the same themes and
characters, the *Iliad* and *Aeneid* are two very different
works. It is widely and wrongly believed that Homer's *Iliad*
tells the story of the Trojan War, whereas it actually only
describes the events of a particularly busy fortnight during
that decade-long conflict. Also the *Iliad* takes a neutral
stance with its protagonists – one can cheer for the noble
Trojan Hector or the doomed Greek Achilles. The point of
the *Iliad* is to tell a good story.

The *Aeneid* also tells a good story, but in this case
the point of the story is to convey a larger message. This
message is that the glory of Rome was preordained, that
the rise to power of Vergil's patron Augustus was the
culmination of an age-old destiny, and Rome had the right,
nay, the duty to rule the known world.

The two epics are separated by more than a thousand years, and social evolution had changed the outlook of the public in that time. No longer was it enough for a hero to be interested only in status, loot and glory (the sole pre-occupations of every male in the *Iliad*). The Romans were nationalists – a concept that simply did not exist in Homer's time. Vergil's Aeneas manages the difficult feat of being a patriot of a Roman state that did not yet exist. Yet this is necessary, for although Vergil set his epic at the time of the Trojan War, his readers lived in a Rome where most of the 'prophecies' in the *Aeneid* had already been fulfilled. The message of the *Aeneid* was that it was right and proper that this should be so.

With this promise in mind, Aeneas and his men now sailed up the coast of Italy to the mouth of the Tiber, where they ran into major problems with chronology. The problem was Ulysses (Odysseus to the Greeks) who, according to the *Aeneid*, was just ahead of the intrepid Aeneas and his crew in his own wanderings. Yet here in Italy, a few miles inland, Aeneas met a son of Ulysses and the hermit witch Circe. Given the timing of the meeting of Ulysses with Circe, that son must have been born within the previous decade. He must have been a highly precocious youth, for when he met Aeneas he was not only an adult but had a grown daughter called Lavinia.

This prodigy was King Latinus, who was to give his name to the Latin people and language as well as the eponym Latium to the area south-east of the Tiber that this people inhabited. Vergil sidestepped the entire problem by ripping Latinus from the parents assigned to him by myth (e.g. in Hesiod's *Theogony*) and fostering him with a new father and mother – the demigod Faunus and a nymph called Marica. This did not really help, because Faunus (says Ovid's *Fasti*) pre-dated by some distance the Aborigines and Evander's city of Pallantium. Therefore, instead of being a child just about adjusting to solid food (as the previous chronology would have had Latinus) Vergil transforms him into a being at least several centuries old. In short, however we try to square Vergil's Latinus with pre-existing legend, it just does not work.

Vergil's version of Latinus was happy to join forces with the newcomers but the rest of his people were not. A nasty little war resulted. Another hero of the Trojan War, the Greek warrior Diomedes, had established a settlement of his own nearby but he firmly indicated that he did not want to get involved. Aeneas went further in his search for allies and ended up at the city of Pallantium beside the Tiber, where Evander gave him a guided tour with many a nod toward future developments that would happen on the site. The Capitoline hill was apparently a thorn-covered outcrop at this time, though the townsfolk already reckoned it sacred to Jupiter.

With the help of his proto-Roman allies from Pallantium Aeneas won his war, even though Evander's son perished in the fighting. The goddess Juno, who had firmly resisted the re-founding of Troy (she had been on the side of the Greeks in the Trojan War) was now reconciled to the fact. She allowed Aeneas the victory, but only on condition that his people took the name and language of the people of Latinus.

These terms were happily accepted. Aeneas married the daughter of Latinus and the Trojans (now Latins) settled in

a town that Aeneas founded as their new home. This town he named Lavinium after his new wife. The 'Trojan' settlement of Lavinium has endured through the ages and remains today a pleasant little town 28 kilometres (17½ miles) south of Rome. Visitors might like to pay particular attention to a very ancient burial site still existing in Lavinium, which Dionysius of Halicarnassus believed to be the tomb of Aeneas. 'It is a small mound, with well-placed rows of trees around it that make it worth a look' (*Roman Antiquities* 1.64.5).

THE NEXT GENERATION

Ancient myth was not immutable, and poets and playwrights had little hesitation in deviating from the accepted version of events if it suited their purposes. With the *Aeneid*, Vergil was actually being relatively conservative – earlier playwrights, such as Euripides, had taken much greater liberties with established myth. Unlike Euripides et al., Vergil did not simply invent his stories wholesale but carefully picked and chose his material from foundation legends and folklore already extant in his time. His adaptations of ancient myths had a dual purpose. Not only did Vergil want to tell as exciting a tale as possible, but his tale needed to suit the propaganda purposes of his master Augustus.

One result of this second purpose was that the son of Aeneas needed to be renamed. Well, re-renamed actually. Apparently the boy started life as Euryleon, but after the fall of Troy his father called him Ascanius, perhaps in honour of a fallen comrade of that name. However, Vergil wanted a direct connection, which confirmed the claim of Augustus that his line was descended directly from the goddess Venus. (This was a claim that Augustus's adoptive father, Julius Caesar, was fond of making.) Therefore Euryleon/Ascanius was reinvented as Iulus, from whom, it was claimed, had originated Rome's Julian family. The historian Livy loyally backs up this claim (in *From the Founding of the City* 1.3.2), though Dionysius of Halicarnassus has Iulus as a son of Ascanius, and therefore a great-grandson of Venus. This was evidently not close enough a divine connection to suit Augustus, who had Vergil move his divine ancestor back a generation.

Aeneas died in action while fighting enemies who resented his foundation of Lavinium. As mentioned previously, Italy in this period was a very unfriendly place, and anyone who held land had to be prepared to fight to keep it. Young Iulus stepped into his father's place but left the administration of Lavinium in the hands of his stepmother.

Iulus had already decided that if the settlement in Italy was to thrive, all the Trojan eggs should not be in a single Lavinian basket. He had already picked out a site where he intended to settle the next generation, which by now consisted of a mix of native Latins, Trojans and children of the intermarriage of both.

The new city foundation was somewhat further inland, and both Livy and Dionysius give a good account of the place, though Dionysius goes into somewhat more detail:

> Alba occupied the space between a mountain and a lake,
> both of which natural defences served as well as walls
> in making the location highly defensible. The mountain
> is both rugged and high and the lake is broad and deep.
> The plain was watered by way of sluices controlling
> outflow from the lake resulting in lands rich in fruits

equal to anything found elsewhere in Italy. This is particularly true of Alban wine, which is sweet, excellent, superior to everything but Falernian.

(*Roman Antiquities* 1.66)

The settlement became known as Alba Longa. The epithet 'Longa' described the elongated nature of the town forced upon it by its location between the mountain and the water. This helped to distinguish this particular Alba from several other Albae in contemporary Italy.

The Palladium

Iulus transferred to his new city several religious icons saved from Troy, foremost of which was an archaic wooden statuette called the Palladium. This statue was allegedly carved by the goddess Athena herself in memory of her dead friend Pallas (whose death Athena took particularly hard because she herself had accidentally caused it in a mythological mishap).

By this account, the Palladium was considerably older than Troy itself, and had been stored for a long time in a temple in Samothrace before King Ilus brought the statue to Troy. In the process Ilus discovered to his cost that the virgin goddess Athena considered the Palladium desecrated if handled by anyone but a virgin female. Ilus was struck blind, but by way of compensation Troy was considered unconquerable for so long as the Palladium remained within the city.

To render Troy vulnerable, the Greek heroes Diomedes and Odysseus sneaked into Troy and stole the Palladium, an act allowed to go unpunished by the strongly pro-Greek Athena. Somehow Aeneas managed to retrieve the precious artefact, possibly through negotiations with Diomedes after both warriors had settled in Italy and abandoned the animosity which had propelled both across the Mediterranean.

In due course, the Palladium was transferred to the Shrine of Vesta in Rome. It was saved from a fire in 241 BC when Rome's top priest, the Pontifex Maximus, Caecilius Metellus threw himself into the flames to retrieve the ancient artefact. However the effigy had been placed in the care of the (exclusively female) Vestal Virgins for a reason. The heroic, but unfortunately male, Caecilius was promptly stricken blind by the ungrateful statue. (This episode is described in detail in Ovid's *Fasti* 6.417ff.)

When Rome became Christian, respect for the Palladium waned. (One Christian writer described it as a 'mere ugly lump of wood'.) What became of the sacred statue is uncertain. An apocryphal tale says that the emperor Constantine transferred the Palladium to his new city on the Bosphorus, and it remains there still, hidden under the remnants of a porphyry pillar somewhere in modern Istanbul.

II
THE BEGINNINGS OF ROME

The great name of Rome is known to all mankind, but not all writers are agreed about from whom or from what circumstances the city was given its name.

(PLUTARCH, *Life of Romulus* 1.1)

There is no single account of the foundation of Rome. Our major sources for the city's early legends are Plutarch, Livy and Dionysius of Halicarnassus (it is likely that Plutarch used Dionysius as one of *his* major sources). All three agree that, in Dionysius's words, 'The Romans don't have a single historian or chronicler from their early days, but each of their [later] historians has extracted something from the ancient accounts' (*Roman Antiquities* 1.73.1). What they extracted was variable, and variably applied, because the later Romans strongly subscribed to two somewhat incompatible ideas. First, they held that their city had had the meanest of beginnings and later generations of Romans had dragged Rome from its squalid origins to its present greatness. Yet they also believed that Rome was a city ordained, promoted and protected by the gods from the beginning. The often conflicting and complex foundation stories reflect the Romans' desire to have their legendary cake and eat it.

Before we explore these alternative legends there is one myth of the founding of Rome which must be dismissed. This is the idea perpetrated by many twentieth-century historians that Rome was not founded at all but grew organically from a few huts at a crossing place by the Tiber into a village, a town and then eventually a mighty city. This version is simply wrong. Certainly, many modern cities have developed through organic growth. But they all lay within already organized nation-states – a small settlement can only grow in this way with the protection of a military force much larger than it can provide for itself. Had early Rome attempted to grow organically in the anarchic and violent conditions of early Iron Age Italy, the place would have lasted just long enough for someone to note that it was worth looting. After that it would have been burned to the ground. The only villages in Iron Age Italy were satellite communities of larger established cities. Furthermore, if Rome had truly evolved from a small hamlet it would have been very much the exception to every other contemporary city in the ancient world. Generally, a new city was born when an existing one had grown to the point at which it was necessary to export some of the surplus population. Dionysius gives a nod to this in one account, claiming that Rome's original settlers from southern Italy included: 'a band of holy youths consecrated to the gods according to local custom. These, they say, were sent off by their elders to find such lands as the gods might give them' (*Roman Antiquities* 2.1.2). This ties in with the *ver sacrum* or 'sacred spring', a rite practised in Italy even into historical times, by which a generation was made sacred to the god Mars and sent from its native city to find a new home.

Beyond doubt, Greek cities outside Greece were founded by colonists, and there is plenty of evidence that this form of expansion happened with other Mediterranean cultures also. Carthage, for example, draws its name from the Phoenician words for 'new city' and historians have no problem believing that Carthage was founded by settlers from Tyre in the

Levant, or that Carthaginians founded cities of their own in Iberia. King Nabonidus of Babylon (556–539 BC) was an early archaeologist with a passion for finding the foundation-stones of cities already ancient in his day. The onus to prove their case, therefore, rests with those who believe that Rome, uniquely, was not founded by a deliberate act but simply grew organically. And such proof does not exist. While both Plutarch and Dionysius cite numerous accounts of the founding of Rome, not one claims that Rome was *autochthonos* (literally 'grown from the earth', the Greek term for a self-evolved city).

Back to the legends. The most basic foundation legend (see p. 17) has a mythical Greek group of colonizers, the Pelasgians, driving the indigenous Sicels from central Italy and founding a city. This city they named 'Rom' from their word for 'strength'. Another version says that displaced returnees from the Trojan War (by some accounts Greek, by others Trojan) took refuge from a violent storm by sailing up the river Tiber. A woman called Roma decided to put an end to their wanderings by conspiring with the other women to burn their ships. Though at first furious, the men soon realized that they had chanced upon an excellent location for a city and named it Roma in recognition of the woman who had stranded them there.

So were the legendary founders indigenous Italians, Greeks or Trojans? Colonists or wandering heroes? Dionysius helpfully offers an account that is a neat omnibus edition of all the existing foundation legends, and which is worth quoting at length for that reason:

> The Aborigines were joined in their settlement with the Pelasgians ... After the Pelasgians came the Arcadians ...

They founded a town by one of the seven hills near the middle of [where] Rome [would later be], calling this town Pallantium, from their mother-city in Arcadia. Not long afterwards, Hercules came into Italy ... and some of the Greeks in his retinue settled near Pallantium, on another of the seven hills. This hill was then called the Saturnian, but now the Romans call it the Capitoline.

...

In the sixteenth generation after the Trojan war the people of Alba Longa united both these places into one city. The Albans themselves were a mixture of Pelasgians, Arcadians, settlers from Elis and, finally, Trojans who came into Italy with Aeneas ... The Greek element was probably diluted with barbarians who either joined the settlement or were the remnants of ancient peoples who were there originally. The combined nations had lost their separate identity and came to be called Latins, after Latinus, the former king of this country.

(*Roman Antiquities* 2.1–2)

The Romans were keen to claim the Trojan part of their heritage, but once they decided that their city had been founded in the eighth century BC, there was a problem. They needed to explain where the descendants of Aeneas had been for the 350 years between the fall of Troy and the launch of Rome. As we have seen, they decided that Iulus/Ascanius founded Alba Longa and thus neatly resolved this issue.

A question which intrigues twenty-first century historians and archaeologists is whether Alba Longa actually existed. Its supposed location is known but cannot be dug up. The hills just outside modern Rome have always been a desirable refuge for urbanites seeking relief from the heat and bustle of the metropolis. Where Alba Longa might have been is now the thriving resort community of Castel Gandolfo and any extensive archaeological work would involve uprooting houses, a venerable villa complex from imperial Roman times, and the palace and extensive gardens of the papal summer retreat. Consequently, for now Castel Gandolfo is keeping its secrets buried beneath its soil.

The Mysterious Etruscans

Besides Aborigines, Pelasgians and Latins, another people to inhabit ancient Italy (and to have an influence on the evolution of Rome) were the Etruscans. While the origins of Rome are well documented (though the veracity of that documentation is another matter), no one really knows anything about the origins or history of the Etruscans. No work by any Etruscan historian has survived to the modern era, so what we know of that people comes from archaeology and asides by other classical writers.

The Greek historian Herodotus reckoned that the Etruscans were a people of Asia Minor who emigrated en masse to Italy in the eighth century BC. Dionysius, on the other hand, thought they were a native Italian people. Modern linguistic research suggests that Dionysius was on the right track. The Etruscan language is as obscure and impenetrable as Etruscan history, but from the little that modern researchers have been able to decipher from surviving inscriptions it appears as though Etruscan may have evolved from languages spoken in prehistoric Italy that were extinct by the Roman era.

An earlier generation of modern historians believed that the Etruscans were a gloomy people preoccupied by death – a viewpoint coloured by the fact that all they had to study of the Etruscans were their graveyards. Modern archaeology has revealed the Etruscans to have had a rich, vibrant culture which was heavily influenced by the trade links which they had established across the Mediterranean world.

After Ascanius/Iulus, Alba's royal dynasty was called Silvian, from the Latin *silva* meaning 'woodland', because the second king, Silvius, spent much of his childhood hiding out in the woods from political rivals. Alba Longa grew into a thriving city, but its location between mountain and lake necessarily limited its size. Therefore the city itself founded a number of colonies, the inhabitants of which later came to be known as the Prisci Latini (the 'old Latins'). Later Romans produced several different king lists for the rulers of Alba Longa, all of whom seem to have had reigns of suspiciously similar lengths of just over twenty-five years. An exception was Tiberinus, who lasted only eight years before he drowned in the river Albula. The manner of his death converted the late king into a riparian demigod, and ever since the Albula has been known as the Tiber. Another monarch of note was Aventinus who was (for some reason) buried on the later site of Rome, giving his name to the Aventine hill.

According to the most commonly accepted legend, the old settlement of Pallantium declined as the city of Alba Longa flourished. By the time of King Proca (*c.* 800 BC) the area beside the Tiber was largely abandoned apart from a hill across the valley from the Palatine. That hill had an abundance of willow trees (*Salix viminalis*) and was occupied by an offshoot of the local Sabine tribe who used the pliant branches to make baskets. It still bears the name derived from these now largely vanished trees: the Viminal. Apart from the Viminal, the historian Livy informs us that 'the countryside thereabouts was substantially wilderness' (*From the Founding of the City* 1.4.6).

The Lupercalia

One memory of ancient Pallantium lingered in Rome – the Arcadian festival of the Lupercalia, which was celebrated on the Palatine hill every year in honour of the god Pan.

While Pan's totemic animal was the goat, the Lupercalia, as the name implies, was a wolf-themed celebration. The festival was celebrated in Rome for over a millennium until the city turned Christian, but ancient writers are probably correct in their belief that this rite was older than Rome itself. The celebration was allegedly so named because Pan had his home on Mount Lycaeus (from the Greek word for wolf) in Arcadia, but the name was adopted enthusiastically because the wolf had a major role in Etruscan religion, and that religion was also strong in Latium. In fact, because the Tiber represented the border between

Etruria and Latium, and the Palatine was situated beside the Tiber, this hill was an excellent place for the celebration of the Latin Lupercalia.

The Lupercalia was at once a fertility and a purification rite and it featured nudity, sex and animal sacrifice. Even later Romans were rather squeamish about some aspects of the ritual, so it is unsurprising that the Christian Church considered the Lupercalia an abomination and banned it outright.

King Proca had two sons, Numitor and Amulius. When Proca passed away (after the standard quarter-century reign) he was briefly succeeded by Numitor, his eldest son. Amulius was not interested in playing second fiddle to his royal brother and seized the throne of Alba Longa for himself. Numitor was forced into retirement on his estate outside the city, but his two sons were assassinated, and his daughter 'promoted' to become a Vestal Virgin. This was no doubt an honour, but also useful for Amulius, who was determined that Numitor's line should become extinct.

The daughter is interesting for several reasons: notably her name, which is given variously as Rhea, Rhea Silvia and Ilia. Rhea was the name of one of the earliest of the Greek goddesses, the daughter of Gaia and mother of the original six Olympian gods, including Zeus. Interestingly, among the original Rhea's totems is the silver fir tree, which brings us back to our unwilling Vestal's alternative name of Silvia, with its woodland connotations. Silvia, of course, also marks the daughter as a legitimate member of the line of Aeneas through Ascanius and Silvius. Some later poets took to calling her Ilia in order to emphasize the link with Ilium (Troy) and the Julian family of Augustus (the *gens Iulia*).

Rhea Silvia/Ilia's story now takes a turn into the kind of deliberate ambiguity that later Roman writers found so handy. Despite her Vestal status, she fell pregnant with twins. If we are to believe the 'squalid' hypothesis of Rome's origins, the father was Rhea Silvia's uncle Amulius, who raped his niece. Rhea Silvia herself, however, promoted the 'divine intent' theory by claiming that she had been impregnated by the god Mars. If it was the will of the gods that she bear the children of Mars, then even her status as a Vestal, with its lifelong vow of virginity, was secondary to her divine destiny.

Mars, incidentally, is an interesting choice of divine father. Later Romans knew Mars as the god of war and, given the formidable strength of Roman arms, it seemed natural to them that their race should claim him as an ancestor. However, in early Rome Bellona was the city's goddess of war and Mars was an agricultural god associated with woodland (that *silva* theme again). It was only when the Romans later realized that Bellona was totally incompatible with the Greek war god Ares that they swapped the axe and shovel of Mars for a shield and sword and thrust this god into the battle line as their Ares equivalent.

So those studying the legend of Rhea Silvia are presented with two versions: she was either raped by her uncle or 'seduced' by Mars. Even in the latter version, as with so many classical tales of divine paternity, there isn't much thought to Rhea Silvia's consent. Livy, whose account of the founding of Rome was generally accepted as definitive, manages neatly to perch between the two stools of 'squalid origin' and 'divine purpose' here:

> I maintain that the Fates decreed the beginning of so great a city and the creation of an empire second only to the gods. Therefore after her rape the Vestal Rhea produced twins. She claimed that Mars was the father of her illegitimate children, either because she believed that to be the truth or because it made her offence less blameworthy if caused by a god.
>
> (*From the Founding of the City* 1.4.1)

Modern readers will be shocked to hear a rape victim described as guilty of an 'offence'. As a Vestal Virgin dedicated to a life of chastity in the service of the goddess Vesta, Rhea Silvia was considered to have broken her vows, even if unwillingly. In the Roman world rape was not just an act of bodily violation against the victim but also an offence against the male guardian responsible for her – or in this case the deity to which Rhea Silvia had pledged herself. The offence, therefore, is considered to have taken place regardless of whether Rhea Silvia was a willing participant or not – indeed, contrary to our modern-day understanding, consent (because it was not hers to give) would have made her *more* 'guilty'. It is important, then, to explore these attitudes in order to understand why Livy's reasoning would not have been controversial to a Roman reader.

Amulius was not going to pass up the chance to have Rhea Silvia imprisoned for breaking her vows to Vesta. Indeed he would have executed her quite happily were it not that, as a usurper, he had to have some consideration for public opinion.

(This was probably why Numitor was still alive.) However, Amulius was certainly not buying the story that Rhea Silvia's twins were sons of Mars – possibly because he himself had been the rapist. Through their mother, the children were of the line of Numitor, which he had been working hard to extirpate. The baby boys had to be killed, and Amulius's chosen method was to throw them into the Tiber – a gesture of contempt as the river served as the local garbage disposal system (and was later used for the disposal of executed criminals). The river was in flood at the time, so the servants charged with disposing of the twins simply dumped the basket into one of the overflow pools and assumed that it would be carried downriver, slowly sink and drown its human cargo.

At this point the twins join a theme so common that it has a name – the legend of the crypto-king. 'Crypto' here means 'secret', because the abandoned child grows up without the palace knowing that the babe is still alive. (Despite the terminology, the crypto-person need not be a king – or a queen for that matter – but merely someone with a far-reaching destiny.) The first known crypto-king was Zeus himself, raised by the goat Amalthea without the knowledge of his cannibalistic father Cronos. Then comes Sargon the Great of Akkad (c. 2340–2280 BC), who allegedly claimed that his mother, a priestess, was forced to dispose of her child 'in a basket sealed with tar, which she cast into the river'. This story, found in a contemporary inscription, goes on to describe how Sargon was found and adopted by a gardener and later came to claim his destiny. The similarities between the stories of Moses and of Rhea's twin children are very noticeable. Other notable crypto-kings of myth and legend include Oedipus, who was thrown

into the wilderness as a babe with his feet bound so tightly that his name means 'swollen foot', King Arthur, Snow White, Cyrus the Great of Persia and Luke Skywalker.

Generally, the crypto-king is adopted by someone of humble origins (though Moses scored a princess), but Rhea's twins were adopted by a wolf. The wolf is an animal highly significant in Etruscan religion, and as Etruscan religion was itself highly significant in the development of Roman religion, the adoption of the twins by a wolf, rather than any other animal, shows that either the gods or early mythologers were working hard on this aspect of the legend. Here again we come to the deliberate ambiguity of the Roman legends. The 'divine plan' version has the twins guided by the river-god Tiberinus to a she-wolf who had lost her cubs. Sheltered in a cave on the slopes of the Palatine she nursed the twins to relieve the pressure on her dugs. A she-wolf was appropriate, because in Roman myth the wolf was the totemic animal of the god Mars. (In Greek mythology the wolf was a symbol of Zeus Lycaeus, and the Romans were happy to accept the Greek interpretation also.) A woodpecker – symbolic of King Picus – kept guard while the twins suckled.

The Capitoline Wolf

Given the controversies surrounding the foundation of Rome it is appropriate that the most famous depiction of the event should itself be controversial. The Capitoline Wolf is a statue that depicts a large she-wolf staring alertly into the distance while a pair of babies crouch beneath suckling at her dugs.

This depiction, incidentally, would suggest that the twins spent a lot of time with mother wolf, because the twins were cast into the river as newborns. To sit up in the manner of the children in the sculpture they would need to be at least ten months old.

It is generally agreed that there were several statues of the wolf and twins in Rome during the classical era. Dionysius describes one such: 'On the side of the Palatine is a sacred precinct with a statue ... which represents a she-wolf suckling two infants. The figures are bronze and of ancient workmanship' (*Roman Antiquities* 1.79.8). Cicero and Pliny the Elder also mention one statue each. The question is whether the Capitoline Wolf is one of these statues. The twins are cast in a totally different style and it is certain they were a later addition during the Renaissance. As to the wolf, it has been variously argued that the statue is sixth-century BC Etruscan (based on the artistic style and copper content) all the way up to twelfth-century Carolingian (based on the casting technique). What is undeniable is that the two contrasting styles of sculpture – the cruder feral wolf, the promise signified by the more sophisticated depiction of the twins – have combined harmoniously to create an evocative and significant work of great art.

Having god-born children escorted to safety by a river deity who found them an appropriate wet-nurse did not work for those pushing the 'squalid origins' theory, so in his history Livy affords these cynics space as well. By both versions of the account, the twins were eventually discovered and adopted by the shepherd Faustulus (Cyrus the Great and Oedipus were also raised by shepherds) who 'gave them to his wife Larentia to raise. Some writers think that Larentia, because she sold her body, was called "the she-wolf" by the shepherds, and the legend arose from this' (Livy, *From the Founding of the City* 1.4.7). Certainly in Livy's Rome a brothel was called a *luparia* or 'she-wolves' den', and for a squalid origin story one can hardly do better than having the children of an incestuous rape escaping murder by their uncle and being raised by a prostitute. Though this version does raise the issue that, if the Palatine hill was largely a wilderness as Livy claims, Larentia could hardly have had a thriving business.

And incidentally, here again we get a possible reason for the name of Rome, for Plutarch (*Life of Romulus* 6) suggests that the children were called *ruma* – the Latin for 'teat' – because they had been breastfed by a wolf.

The twins, named Romulus and Remus, grew into young men who naturally became leaders of the local youth. Romulus, in particular, developed a certain notoriety because of the ruffians and toughs whose company he seemed to prefer. Nevertheless, it was Remus who first got into serious trouble. This was because someone attacked and looted the estate of Numitor – by some accounts bandits, by others servants of Amulius. In either case, the twins and their band of happy desperadoes launched an ambush and looted the looters. The twins' victims bided their time until Romulus and Remus were separated. Then, when Remus was attending the rite of the Lupercalia on the Palatine hill, the robbers seized him. With a certain warped irony, they took Remus to Numitor, claiming that they had captured one of the men who had looted his estate, and by way of proof had found the booty in his possession and that of his brother Romulus. Numitor questioned the captive and heard the story of the brothers' abandonment in a basket on the river Tiber. Since the last that Numitor had heard of his grandchildren was that they had been thrown into the Tiber in a basket, it was not hard for him to put the story together.

Romulus, meanwhile, had assembled a rescue mission for his brother, but when his adoptive father Faustulus revealed the truth of the twins' origins he converted this to a rescue mission for his imprisoned mother. (Plutarch and Livy do not subscribe to the darker version of the tale given by Dionysius, in which Rhea Silvia was found guilty of being unchaste and beaten to death, and her body cast into the Tiber.) Remus turned up at Alba Longa with a force of Numitor's servants at the same time as Romulus launched his attack. Taking their cue from this, the people of the city joined in to overthrow the unpopular Amulius. So this part of the legend comes to a fairy-tale ending. The evil Amulius was slain, Rhea Silvia was freed to embrace her long-lost children and Numitor again ascended his rightful throne. Plutarch for one was suspicious of this happily-ever-after conclusion, and remarks dubiously:

> Fabius [Pictor – reputed to be Rome's first historian] says things transpired in this way. So does Diocles of Peparethus, who seems to have been the first to write a description of the founding of Rome. There are those who consider the story too fantastic to be anything but fiction or fable. Yet why should we doubt when we see that fate can indeed express itself almost poetically?

II

Also consider that Rome could not have reached its present greatness were it not of divine origin, and events influenced by the gods generally include marvels.

(Life of Romulus 8.7)

The last word goes to posterity. Numitor later gave his name to a US Navy warship, while 'Amulius' has joined a genus of predatory insects known as 'assassin bugs'.

III

CHILDREN OF THE WOLF

Rome was, according to tradition, founded at 11 a.m. on 21 April 753 BC. One cannot fault the ancient Romans' precision. They calculated the period between the foundation of their city and the end of Rome's western Empire, therefore, as being 1,229 years, 135 days and about 13 hours. (Any Roman beginning a legend with 'once upon a time ...' would have quickly lost his audience. The Romans wanted exact dates, names and places.) There's a degree of inexactitude here, because we do not know the time of day on that fateful 4 September AD 476 at which Romulus Augustulus, Rome's last emperor, was informed that he had lost his job. Nevertheless, Rome's impeccably neat record of timekeeping for over a millennium will be hard for any future empire to surpass.

Given the murky circumstances surrounding the origin of Rome one might be forgiven for looking with considerable scepticism at the exactitude of the city's foundation date. This scepticism becomes downright disbelief when one realizes that the consensus for this date only became established after Rome had been a going concern for over 700 years. Some of the earliest chroniclers of Rome's history put the foundation almost immediately after the Trojan War, while the first native Roman historian, one Fabius Pictor, opted for 747 BC. For a while opinion seemed to coalesce around 751 BC, the date selected by Cato the Elder, and supported by his contemporary the great Greek historian Polybius.

Plutarch, who wrote a biography of Romulus, seems to have assumed that Rome's founder did the deed in 753 BC. His opinion was based on what are today called the Capitoline *Fasti*.

These are a set of records, carved on marble tablets, which listed by year all the major magistracies of the Roman state, but especially the kings and later the consuls. (The consuls were chief magistrates, elected annually, who wielded near-kingly powers during the Roman Republic.) This was important because the Romans usually referred to a year by the name of whosoever was in charge at the time. Later the Romans used A.U.C. (*Ab urbe condita*) – the year since the founding of the city. However, this latter measurement was only possible once opinion had coalesced around a year when the founding happened and that year was – by today's measure – Plutarch's choice of 753 BC.

The Parilia

The Parilia was a rural festival of purification sacred to the goddess Pales. This was the time for cleansing away the penalties for impieties such as inadvertently cutting branches from a sacred grove or watering cattle in a sacred spring. The rites of that day included shepherds and their livestock jumping through the flames of burning straw. The poet Ovid remarks, 'We jump through flames on Rome's birthday as did farmers who set fire to the cottages they were abandoning as they went to found Rome' (*Fasti* 4.805ff).

Oddly enough, while the year was uncertain for several centuries, the day and the month – 21 April – was firmly established. This is because it was agreed from the start that Rome was founded on the date of the Parilia. This festival was older than Rome – some believed it was established by Aeneas himself – and certainly it would be considered an auspicious day for the peoples of an agricultural community to found a new settlement.

While we have explored some of the legends of the origins of Rome, there is only one major legend of the founding itself. This is the story of how Romulus came to establish his city on that bright spring morning of the fourth year of the sixth Olympiad.

Keeping Time with the Olympics

By tradition the first Olympic Games were held in the year 776 BC and every four years thereafter. In a world where every city had its own calendar and began its year at an arbitrary date, it was important to have one set of dates that everyone agreed upon. Thanks to the Greek habit of settling everywhere across the Mediterranean, everyone in their proximity knew when the Olympics took place and which Olympiad (that is, one iteration of the Games) had most recently occurred. Therefore, one could refer to an Olympiad and the years that followed it to produce a date in the past upon which everyone could agree.

FOUNDATION

The legend of the founding relates that once the dust had settled in Alba Longa with the death of the wretched Amulius and the restoration of Numitor to his throne, Romulus and Remus had to decide what to do next with their lives. Now that they were revealed as princes of the line of Aeneas they could hardly go back to being shepherds, but given their active upbringing they were not prepared to sit around and wait for Numitor to vacate his throne by dying of old age.

It occurred to them that the site of the abandoned city of Pallantium was crying out for resettlement. There were a number of advantages to the location. Firstly, thanks to the Tiber, the place had easy access to the sea. This meant that the new city would have contact with the rest of the Mediterranean world but without the risks of a settlement right on the coast. (As an example of those hazards, as late as the first century BC, when Rome was mistress of a mighty empire, her port city of Ostia was nevertheless attacked and devastated by pirates.)

In fact, Rome was at what modern geographers call the 'head of navigation', which is about as far as sea-going ships can sail upriver without getting into difficulty. (Modern London is located at this same point on the Thames.) One reason that ships could not get any further up the Tiber was because a volcanic ridge made this the nearest point to the coast at which the river could be forded. This was important, because it meant that the proposed settlement of Romulus would sit squarely across the already ancient Via Salaria – a long-established trade route by which salt extracted from the pans at Ostia was brought to the Italian interior.

Considered objectively, the proposed site consisted of three hills alongside the Tiber (those later called the Capitoline, the Palatine and the Aventine) separated by a valley from a long ridge (later divided into the Quirinal, Viminal and Esquiline hills) with the low bump of the Caelian hill at the south end of the valley. Regrettably, there was no equivalent of the Caelian at the north end, so the valley (later the site of the Roman

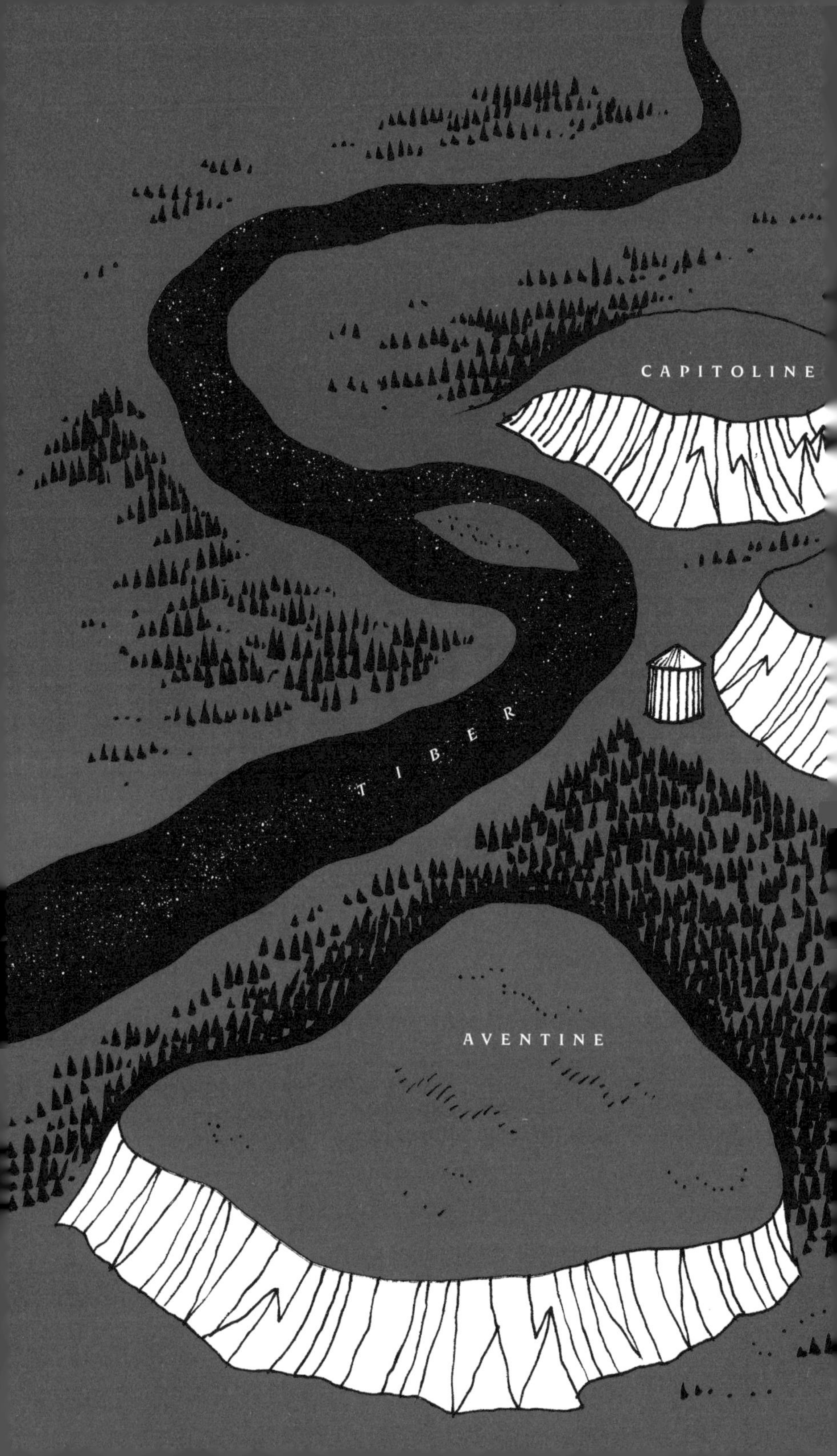
CAPITOLINE
TIBER
AVENTINE

QUIRINAL

VIMINAL

ESQUILINE

PALATINE

CAELIAN

Forum) tended to act as an overflow route when the Tiber was in flood.

Since the east ridge was already occupied by the Sabine tribe – who were none too happy to see the new arrivals – this left the hills beside the Tiber. The Capitoline could be ruled out because its slopes were steep and craggy, so the choice was between the Palatine and the Aventine hills. Romulus wanted the Palatine, but there are diverging traditions for the choice of Remus. Some, including the ancient writer Festus, believe that his proposed settlement was on a hill some 8 kilometres (5 miles) downstream of the Tiber from the Palatine, but the legend which later became the established version has Remus choosing the Aventine.

Many Romans believed that the brothers each intended to establish their own cities on their favoured hills, but the more common tradition is that the pair agreed to let the gods decide where the new settlement should be situated. So on the day of the Parilia Remus took up station on the Aventine to consult the auspices. The gods had many ways of signalling their will to a watcher of the skies, but the most common was divination through the flight of birds. Of these avian phenomena the vulture was the most prestigious so Remus must have been delighted to observe that the gods had sent not one but six of these birds.

When given the news of his brother's sighting, Romulus retorted that the gods had sent him twelve vultures – though in fact he had seen none. Vultures tend to fly at altitude, so twelve birds appearing in the patch of sky allocated to Romulus for his divination would also have been visible from the Aventine – especially as tradition locates the observation point of Remus

at the top of that hill. Even from that prominence the vultures of Romulus had not been seen, which made his claim highly suspect. It did not help matters that, when an indignant Remus came to confront Romulus with his lie, the twelve vultures then made a belated appearance – handing the win to Romulus with his brother as an extremely discomfited witness.

Plutarch on Vultures

Plutarch gives the following account of vultures in *Life of Romulus* 9.5–7:

According to [the writer] Herodorus Ponticus even Hercules was happy if a vulture turned up during the course of one of his Labours. The vulture does less harm than any other animal – it damages no crops, orchards or livestock but lives on creatures already dead. That which is living it does no harm and other birds being of its own kind, the vulture does not touch them even when dead. Eagles, owls, and hawks attack other birds and kill them, so as [the playwright] Aeschylus says, 'How can one consider pure a bird that preys on other birds?'

Furthermore, most birds are always before our eyes, so to speak – they pop up all the time. But a vulture is a rare sight. As to the young, they are so hard to discover that some suspect that these birds come from another land and only visit here as adults. Even then so sporadic are their appearances that soothsayers believe that these are never natural or spontaneous but always manifested by the divine.

While Remus stalked back to rejoin his followers on the Aventine, Romulus started laying out his new city. At this time his chosen hill was not called the Palatine. That was the name of one of the two peaks which rose on the north and south sides of the hill. (The other peak was called the Cermalus.) Between the Palatine peak and the Cermalus was a small plateau some 40 metres (130 feet) above the Tiber, which was around 10 hectares (25 acres) in size. Romulus intended to lay out his city in a grid pattern on this plateau, a settlement to which later Romans attributed the name 'Roma Quadrata'.

Since the hill had its own water supply from several natural springs and had relatively steep sides, it was easily defensible. Nevertheless, Romulus as his first order of business set about constructing walls to enclose his settlement. As mentioned earlier, Rome was on the border with Etruria, and lay across a valuable trade route. The only things that would prevent his new city from being crushed immediately by its neighbours would be sound defences and the fact that Latin shepherds were a particularly recalcitrant bunch who owned little that was worth the hard fighting needed to take it from them.

With the fast-growing population of early Iron Age Italy, new settlements were not uncommon. As a result one did not just throw up walls willy-nilly. Tradition and religion had established certain protocols. These walls on the Palatine were also to be Rome's *pomerium* – a sacred boundary the crossing of which was punishable by death. Romulus set about marking these boundaries with a plough. As tradition dictated, the ploughshare was of bronze and pulled by an ox and a cow. Romulus carefully lifted his plough in three places (since an impermeable sacred boundary would rapidly condemn those within to death by starvation). Each gap in the *pomerium* was to become a gate into the city. The number of gates was three, in accordance with the Etruscan tradition. We know the names given to two of these gates from later writings. The main gate was the Porta Romana, and the other the Porta Mugonia. The third gate was later absorbed into the structure of the growing city and its name and location lost to posterity.

From the moment that Romulus marked the *pomerium* with his furrow anyone who crossed that line in the loam was automatically a *hostis* – an enemy of the city. Behind the plough of Romulus the other settlers were already hard at work turning the furrow into a rampart. Meanwhile, on the Aventine Remus was busily doing the same, for his party maintained that the gods favoured their hill on account of the vultures having appeared first to Remus.

It would be fair to describe relations between the twins as extremely tense at this point. Things got steadily worse because the embittered Remus was intent not only on building his own walls on the Aventine but also on obstructing the work of his cheating brother on the Palatine. At one point Remus was so far ahead that he felt able to mock the efforts of Romulus by leaping over the feeble rampart that was all that the Palatine had to offer in the way of defences.

The problem was that leaping over the rampart was a violation of the *pomerium*. Celer, a follower of Romulus, then demonstrated the legalistically bloody-minded attitude that was later to distinguish the inhabitants of the city. He immediately declared Remus a *hostis* and cut him down on the spot. A violent fracas followed which left several dead, including Faustulus and his brother, the adoptive father and uncle of the

twins. A remorseful Romulus had Remus interred on his chosen hill of the Aventine at a site which was well known in antiquity as the Remoria, but of which only the approximate location is known today (somewhere near the Basilica di Santa Balbina).

Celer wisely fled the scene of the crime – indeed so fast did he escape to Etruria that his name became a byword among the Romans for speed (*celeritas*). The killer remains with us today in the words 'celerity' and 'accelerate'.

Still with defence in mind, Romulus selected three thousand men to form the city's defence corps. From the Latin *legere*, meaning to 'gather' or 'select' (whence comes the English 'delegate') this body of picked men was called a 'legion'.

So much for the legend. In the 1990s, archaeologists excavating the Palatine found blocks of red tufa that could have been part of a city wall. This was further confirmed by the discovery of a man-made gully running outside of the blocks, which thus created the ditch-and-wall defences of the Villanovan (early Iron Age) culture contemporary with the foundation legend.

Some archaeologists promptly claimed that this was a strong indication that the accounts in ancient literature had a foundation (so to speak) in reality. After all, the archaeologists had dug where the ancient literature had said the walls would be and indeed the walls were there. Sceptics point out that ancient Rome has buried walls in abundance and finding these does not necessarily prove much. Nor is there anything apart from the coincidence of time to suggest that these are the walls of Romulus. The controversy rumbles on, with books such as *Rome: Day One* by Andrea Carandini (who conducted the original excavations) strongly supporting the veracity of the ancient accounts while others indignantly refute the entire idea.

THE SABINES

The legend of the founding once again propounds the Roman idea that theirs was originally a city of scoundrels, but one ordained by the gods. Romulus obtained the sanction of the gods for his city by the divine manifestation of twelve vultures. Then he promptly got events back on their usually sordid track by committing fratricide, to add to the incest and murder which had already given colour (usually crimson) to the foundation legend. Nevertheless those telling the tale decided to add even more violence to the narrative with mass kidnapping and rape.

At this point, although Rome had been a going concern for just four months, the city of Romulus was expanding rapidly. This was because Romulus opened a temple to the god Asylaeus on the Mount of Saturn (as the Capitoline hill was then called). As was the case with many temples, this one allowed individuals to seek sanctuary within. Generally in the ancient world sanctuary was extended to those who had offended the laws of the city where the temple was built. Romulus instead allowed anyone from anywhere in Italy to find shelter and redemption at his temple. Named after the temple's patron god, this Roman version of sanctuary was called 'asylum'.

Soon Rome had a fine citizen body that included wanted criminals, escaped slaves, fortune-seekers, reneging debtors and discharged mercenaries. (The latter, *metelli* in Latin, were probably the founders of later Rome's great family of the Caecilii Metelli.) While a growing population was all well and good, that population consisted almost exclusively of bachelors – and not eligible bachelors either, as Romulus quickly found out.

71

His embassies seeking wives were rejected by nearby communities horrified at the thought of marrying into the gang of ruffians on the Palatine. There may also have been the hope that the city of Rome might be formidable for only a single generation. Without wives the men would have no children and the aged population of Rome would fade from existence like an undernourished and putrescent bloom.

Still, Romulus seemed determined to make a go of things while he yet had a city. He was understandably eager to locate the cave at the base of the Palatine where he and his brother had spent part of their infancy being reared by a she-wolf. This cave – later called the Lupercal – was duly located. (It has been rediscovered in the twenty-first century and its embellishments by later generations of Romans are being enthusiastically picked over by archaeologists.) However, in the process of locating the Lupercal another oddity was discovered.

This was a very ancient shrine dedicated to the god Consus. Nobody was quite sure who the divine Consus was, but the Romans were certainly not going to upset a deity so close to their city. Instead Romulus decreed a day of celebration and athletic events to celebrate the discovery of the shrine and its enigmatic god. This party was to take place in the valley between the Aventine and Palatine hills where the shrine had been discovered. Everyone was invited to attend, and the nearest neighbours of the Romans, the Sabines of the Viminal hill, arrived in large numbers.

The original celebrations for Consus were a cover for a deeper purpose that Romulus had carefully planned – the capture, forcible marriage and rape of any unmarried women who attended the event. Generally in the ancient Mediterranean one could distinguish between wives and maidens (all young women – theoretically at least – fell into one of these two categories) by their hairstyle and dress. During the dancing, singing and athletic events the Roman men carefully marked out their prey and stationed themselves nearby. Others took up position near the Sabine menfolk most likely to offer resistance and prepared to overpower them should they try.

Chariot Races for Consus

The celebrations in honour of Consus were real – indeed the Romans were to repeat those celebrations very regularly for the next thousand years. The flat open space between the Aventine and Palatine was ideal for chariot racing, one of the premier spectator sports of antiquity. These races in the valley were dedicated to Consus, whose shrine was kept covered unless chariot competitions were taking place.

In time, the hillside upon which spectators sat was supplemented with regular seating, and a barrier (*spina*) down the middle of the racecourse was added to prevent collisions between chariots coming and going between the different turning posts. The resultant structure – the Circus Maximus – was among the largest in Rome. At its peak the Circus could seat well over a hundred thousand spectators. Romulus would have been proud and awed, but not necessarily surprised.

III

The Roman poet Ovid takes up the tale in his salacious poem, *The Art of Love* (1.107ff):

> The audience sat on benches cut into the turf, shading
>   their uncombed hair as best they could with leaves.
> They too were watched as each picked out the girl he
>   desired, his heart quietly aflutter.
> While the dancer on the levelled earth floor tapped her
>   feet to the triple-beat tune played on a crude Etruscan
>   flute, the King gave the signal [by raising his cloak,
>   according to Livy]
> Amid the applause they shouted their intent as they
>   sprang upon the women to seize them
> The maidens run in panic from the outlaws like doves
>   from an eagle, like lambs from a predatory wolf.
> All are terrified, but there's no one face of fear. Some
>   tear their hair, others wait in silence knowing all is lost
> She mourns quietly, this one calls helplessly for her
>   mother. She runs, she stays, this one screams,
>   another faints
> ...
> Should one fight to deny her would-be lover, he would
>   hold her tight against his chest and ask
> 'Why streak your gentle cheeks with tears? As was your
>   father to your mother, I'll be with you.'

This was the infamous Rape of the Sabines, an event which has been depicted in art many times: by the Romans themselves, by medieval and Renaissance artists, and by modern film-makers. It is important to note that, here, 'rape' does not mean sexual assault in the strictest physical definition. Rather this is an ancient sense of the word from the Latin *raptus*, meaning 'violently seized' – it is from the same root that hawks and eagles are called 'raptors'. Nevertheless, the women were forcibly carried off and later compelled to marry their captors, submit to sex and bear children to them – a violation by any name.

It says a lot about the ancient Romans that they were rather proud of their actions. In the first century BC the moneyer Lucius Titurius Sabinus struck a coin depicting the event, which, as his name indicates, involved his supposed ancestors. Stealing brides was not uncommon in ancient Italy or pre-classical Greece. Bands of young men might descend upon an unsuspecting village seeking to pillage not just cattle but also wives. Indeed, the original reason why the groom stands to the right of the bride in modern Western weddings is to keep his sword arm free to deal with any outraged in-laws who might intervene.

The modern West has also adopted the Roman tradition of carrying the bride across the threshold. This was originally to symbolize the fact that the first Roman brides – the Sabine women – did not come willingly. In his defence, Romulus might have pointed out that in his day many a girl was an unwilling bride. Women had little say in whom they married. Even in the classical era a girl might only meet her future husband after the engagement and wedding date had already been decided. Romulus probably argued that it made no difference if a husband selected a wife because of family financial and dynastic arrangements or because she happened to catch his eye at a festival.

To the Sabine men the difference certainly mattered – a lot. They had not liked the Romans much to begin with and had only attended the festival to keep things civil. The unwritten rules of hospitality had been grossly violated, and there was the matter of outraged masculine pride as well as genuine grief at the loss of loved daughters and sisters. And yet, while hostilities commenced immediately, open warfare had to wait. We know from the date given by Livy that this was early September. The crops had to be brought in and winter wheat sown, or both Romans and Sabines would starve by the opening of the campaigning season in March.

In addition, the Romans might be a bunch of despicable thugs, rapists and woman-stealers but no one doubted that these desperadoes would fight hard. They also had a sound defensive position. Therefore the Sabine king, a man called Titus Tatius, sent out embassies to other branches of the Sabine tribe and to anyone else who – in the traditionally predatory manner of Italian communities of the time – fancied a chance at attacking and pillaging Roman lands. Furthermore, not just Sabine women but girls from other communities had been abducted at the festival. According to Dionysius, over 683 women were taken (*Roman Antiquities* 2.30.6). Some of these probably came from the nearby city of Caecina, whose people did not wait for the Sabines to get their act together but immediately launched a massive raid.

The raiders underestimated the rapidity and ferocity of the Roman response. 'The enemy were widely scattered as they pillaged and destroyed' remarks Livy (*From the Founding of the City* 1.10.4), when Romulus descended upon them with an organized army that not only put the attackers to flight but also chased them in a disorganized mob back to their city, which the Romans took in their first assault. Romulus personally killed the Caecinian king.

Afterwards 'as anxious to proclaim his deeds as he had been to perform them', Romulus took his spoils back to the Capitoline hill and there vowed a temple to Jupiter 'where posterity shall follow my example by bringing the spoils taken from enemy kings and chieftains slain in battle' (Livy again, 1.10.5).

The Romans were keenly aware that they had within their city a fifth column in the form of outraged women who would be more than happy to see their kidnappers' heads displayed on pikes around their own walls. In fact, one woman was already plotting a devastating blow against the new city. Her name was Tarpeia.

IV

KING ROMULUS

OF LOVE AND WAR

Romulus was well aware of the risk that the new Sabine brides presented to his community, or so Livy tells us. Accordingly he embarked on a round of what is today called 'love-bombing':

> Romulus personally went to them [the women] and argued that it was the women's parents who were responsible for what had happened, because in their pride they had refused the right of intermarriage to their neighbours. Yet as wives their daughters would nevertheless become equal partners in all that the Romans owned, including that dearest possession of all the human race – their children.
>
> They should therefore cool their anger and give their hearts to those to whom fortune had given their persons. Every husband would try all the harder because of this [how he had gained his wife], so the women should moderate their fury with the thought that a sense of outrage can often change to one of affection. Each man was determined to do his best not only to be a good partner but also by his actions to compensate his wife for the home and parents she had lost.
>
> The arguments were supplemented by the earnest courtship of the men who said they had acted only from love and passion – the pleas most calculated to win a woman's heart.
>
> (*From the Founding of the City* 1.9.14–16)

Romulus did not need to add what everyone already knew. If we are to go by the attitude of Romans in later years, it was a bitter truth that once a woman had been raped she was considered 'damaged goods'. Even if the Sabine women were returned to their parents, those parents would be unlikely to find husbands for their daughters. No self-respecting Sabine man would want them. In the opinion of those in the ancient world, one might sympathize with victims but one certainly did not want to associate with them. Victims were either imprudent, and therefore untrustworthy; unlucky, a quality that might be contagious or inflict collateral damage; or hated by the gods, in which case the only solution was to get as far away from them as possible.

In short, as the reluctant brides well knew, they were either going to be Roman wives or spinster outcasts. It might be unfair and unreasonable but perhaps they could make the best of a bad situation and at least give the Romans a chance?

Between wooing their unwilling brides, the Roman menfolk were busy fighting a series of battles with the neighbours who, noting that Rome seemed vulnerable, had taken the chance to gang up on the city. The attackers were surprised and dismayed by the quality of the Roman response. Several other cities followed the precedent of the Caeninensians, a people who opportunistically declared war on the Romans. Each hostile army was defeated in the field, with the Romans following up this rout by attacking their opponents' home city.

So far, this outbreak of warfare was a standard Italian inter-city interaction of the time. But what happened next was unusual. Romulus did not massacre or enslave the conquered townspeople, but instead congratulated them on becoming, like the Sabine brides, new Roman citizens. The conscripted citizens were ordered to pack up their homes and make their way to Rome, where new quarters were found for them on the Palatine. That settlement was already expanding down to the valley, which would later become the Forum. The Romans were also busily fortifying the Mount of Saturn (which would later become the Capitoline) as their citadel of last resort.

While the terrifyingly efficient Roman army devastated the farmlands of their remaining enemies, Romulus took care to leave intact the farmsteads of the in-laws of his new citizens. He himself had taken a Sabine bride, a woman called Hersilia. There are various traditions about Hersilia. Some claimed she was the daughter of Titus Tatius and, alone of the kidnappees, she had been married at the time of her abduction. However, Hersilia had refused to abandon her daughter and had been taken to the city along with the rest. There she had caught the eye of Romulus himself and in marrying him had unilaterally divorced her previous husband. Evidently Hersilia had not been that enamoured of her earlier spouse, for she became an enthusiastic Roman and doubtless persuaded others by her example.

Meanwhile the Sabines had been suffering the opprobrium of their neighbours. These had all tried taking on the Romans, sometimes as individual cities and sometimes collectively. Those that had not retired from the fray with bloody noses had instead been forcibly relocated from their homes to join Rome's swelling population, while the Sabines had merely sent embassies to the Romans asking for the return of their daughters (who were hostages, from one perspective) and offering terms for peaceful co-habitation if this were done.

Only when Romulus explained that Rome was keeping the Sabine women and this was non-negotiable did Titus Tatius plan serious hostilities.

TARPEIA

Central to the plans of Titus Tatius was young Tarpeia. There are various descriptions of this maiden. Some relate that she was among the Sabine women kidnapped by the Romans. Others dispute this, because Tarpeia was undoubtedly a Roman Vestal Virgin and as an abductee would not have been placed in such a position of trust. A rival tradition, therefore, makes Tarpeia the daughter of the commander of the Capitoline garrison. In either case Tarpeia was prepared to betray Rome. Her motive has been variously described as any one of the unholy trinity of treason.

Some felt it was revenge. If she was indeed a Sabine kidnap victim, then Tarpeia's motive was evident and laudable enough. Others argued for lust, for if Tarpeia was a Roman citizen another explanation had to be found. Some claimed that Tarpeia was enamoured of a Sabine youth and felt that the only way she could escape her compulsory virginity in Rome was for Rome to no longer exist. Other ancient writers opted for the oldest and simplest reason of all – greed.

One of Tarpeia's duties as a Vestal Virgin was to fetch water to the shrine of the goddess Vesta. This water had to be from an unsullied spring, in this case the one later called the Carmentine. This was located a fair distance from both the Roman and Sabine settlements. Because her sacred status made her untouchable by either side in the conflict Tarpeia was able to come and go freely. This allowed her to contact the

Sabines and strike a deal whereby she would let them into the city provided the warriors gave her 'what was on their left arms'.

In a world without banking and in which a lack of decent locks made storage under a mattress impracticable, most men carried their wealth around with them in the form of gold bracelets. Since these rather interfered with the operation of a sword arm, this portable wealth usually decorated a warrior's left arm, which was tucked behind his shield during combat.

An aristocratic writer called Piso disagreed with this theory and claimed that Tarpeia had a different motive – patriotism. He reckoned that her compact with the Sabines was deliberately ambiguous and Tarpeia aimed to hold the Sabines to their promise by demanding their shields, thus leaving the enemy at a severe disadvantage in the pitched battle that was to come.

In any case, as arranged, the Sabines silently approached the citadel at night and Tarpeia opened a gate for them. Titus Tatius was the first to give her what was on his left arm. That is, he stunned the girl with a mighty whack of his shield. The other Sabines followed suit, hurling their shields upon the traitorous Tarpeia until she was either killed by the impact or suffocated by the weight. This, the Sabines felt, was suitable punishment for a traitor, however helpful that traitor may have been to them. A cynic (such as Dionysius of Halicarnassus) might note that a dead Tarpeia had little use for Sabine gold, so killing her allowed them to renege on their expensive deal.

The girl's body was then tossed off the steep cliff on the side of the path leading to the gate, and thereafter the Sabines captured the Roman stronghold almost without a fight. So easily did the place fall that Tarpeia's father was also condemned for treason. However, Piso also notes that Tarpeia's body was buried with honours befitting a dead Vestal, and for years after some Roman women sacrificed in her name. This would not have been done for a traitor. Therefore, as Dionysius of Halicarnassus remarks, 'let everyone make of the incident what they will' (*Roman Antiquities* 2.40.3).

The Tarpeian Rock

If Tarpeia was indeed a traitor, this would account for the later use of the precipice from which her body was flung: a cheap means of execution for traitors, who were hurled to their deaths from the heights. Since there were not that many traitors, parricides and thieving slaves were also punished in the same way. (It is recorded that, in the first century BC, when a slave betrayed his master to the blood-thirsty dictator Sulla, the dictator kept his word and gave him the promised reward. He then had the man hurled from the rock for larcenous and traitorous behaviour. The ghost of Tarpeia was probably waiting at the bottom to sympathize.)

In later years this mode of execution was abandoned, less from scruple than because the Forum below was a busy place and people resented the delays and mess caused by falling bodies.

SHOWDOWN, INTERRUPTED

The next day the Romans prepared to retake the Capitol and the Sabines prepared to stop them. The two groups squared off in the valley between their respective settlements for what both foresaw would be the decisive battle. Titus Tatius must have felt the odds were in his favour. The drawn-out Sabine muster had brought in other Sabines from further afield to supplement those Sabines living on the Viminal, so the riffraff of Romulus were outnumbered.

The battle took place in what was later the heart of imperial Rome, and a number of mementoes of that battle remained in the Forum through much of the city's subsequent history. There was, for example, the Lacus Curtius. Later merely a simple monument, this was in Romulus's time a marshy pool with very deep mud at the bottom. Mettius Curtius, a Sabine champion, found this out the hard way when he charged his horse at the Romans. His horse got stuck in the mud and the rest of the Sabine army watched in horror as the animal slowly submerged into the bog – although according to Livy, young Curtius survived the harrowing experience.

While in the thick of the combat Romulus was hit on the head by a stone and his demoralized troops fell back, taking their stunned leader with them. By the time Romulus recovered the Romans had been pushed almost out of the valley and were making a stand on a low hill called the Velia. Even that position looked tenuous. Romulus, still believing in the city's divine destiny, called upon Jupiter to strengthen the crumbling Roman battle line:

Jupiter, through your auspices I founded here beyond
this gate [the Mugonian] your city on the Palatine.
The Sabines have bribed their way into the citadel and
are now forcing us from the valley. Father of the Gods,
remove the fear from Roman hearts and stop a shameful
rout. I vow a temple built right at this place, dedicated

to Jupiter Stator [the Stayer], so that future generations
will know that it is here that you saved Rome.

(LIVY, *From the Founding of the City* 1.12.4–6)

The *Gens* Curtia

Certainly at least one member of Curtius's clan must have
come out of the battle intact, for the family were established
as minor aristocrats in Rome by the time reliable records
exist. Only one of the family attained the consulship, and
that early in the history of the city.

Nevertheless it was probably the influence of the
Curtii that led to a later and altogether more satisfactory
legend about the Lacus to replace that of the rather
ignominious fate of young Mettius. By this account a large
chasm appeared in the Forum. Soothsayers predicted
that this would evidently spread and doom Rome unless
a human sacrifice was cast within. The Romans did
occasionally sacrifice humans, even in historical times, but
they were definitely squeamish about the practice. They
dithered until Curtius (in this version a Marcus) mounted
his steed, rode headlong into the abyss and saved Rome.

The prayer worked, perhaps because the Romans believed it
would, and the Roman line held. Romulus accordingly founded
his temple. Its location is now uncertain, but it was certainly
standing in imperial times, allowing the poet Ovid to give us
a hint:

From there look to your right by the gate of the Palatine.
This is the [Temple of Jupiter] Stator, here where Rome
was born.

(*Tristia* 3.1.31)

Rebuffed at the Velia, the Sabines tried assaulting Rome at
the other end of the valley. They had succeeded in forcing their
way within the walls when the doors of the Temple of Janus
suddenly burst open. (Janus, it will be remembered, was one of
the primordial deities who was believed to have ruled the area
literally at the dawn of time. Unsurprisingly, since they were on
his land, the Romans had built a temple to him as one of their
first actions after founding the city.) A flood of boiling water
poured from the temple and bowled over the Sabines. In the
face of this clear evidence of divine partisanship the scalded
attackers beat a hasty retreat.

After these bruising encounters the battle was at a stale-
mate. Then, before the two sides could re-engage, a third force
joined the fray. This was the Sabine women, several carrying
with them the babies conceived since their abduction. With the
considerable moral authority gained from their suffering they
proceeded to hector both sides alike. One harangue delivered
to the Sabine side was imagined by Plutarch as running thus:

> What harm have we done that we had to suffer for it in
> the past, and are now suffering again?

> First we were lawlessly kidnapped and violated. Then,
> then we were abandoned by our kinsfolk until time
> eventually joined us by the strongest of bonds to those
> whom once we most hated ... No one came to rescue us

while we were virgins, but now you tear husbands from their wives and fathers from their children – a rescue even worse than your former abandonment.

(*Life of Romulus* 19.3–4)

The Temple of Janus

The writer Varro records that there were once hot volcanic springs in the area of the Temple of Janus (*On the Latin Language* 5.156) and this might have been the origin of the legend. Of course, it is also possible that a hot spring was trapped near the temple floor under a thin layer of rock, and hundreds of armoured men charging about caused the rock to crack open.

Thereafter, the Romans decreed that the gates of Janus's temple should remain open if Rome was at war and be closed in times of peace. These gates probably rusted in place, for they were closed only once in the long history of the Republic, in 253 BC.

The argument had its effect and the Sabines agreed to a ceasefire while they checked the living conditions of their daughters for themselves. Once it was seen that the women did indeed have the status of respectable matrons, relationships on the battlefield became a lot more amicable.

The place where Romans and Sabines came to the realization that, like it or not, they were now family, was thereafter called the *comitium*, from the Roman word for 'fellowship'. This

is where, in later ages, the assembly of the plebs (the plebeians, the lower classes of Rome) would meet. *Comitium* evolved to mean an assembly and today the word is one suggested etymology for the term 'committee'.

The terms of the Romano-Sabine peace treaty stated that any woman still unsatisfied with her domestic life could return to her parents. (This remained the case among the patricians in Republican Rome, when a women could consider herself divorced if she remained continuously outside the matrimonial home for three days and then informed her ex-husband that she had done so for the purpose of terminating the marriage.)

The Sabines agreed to join the Romans, merging the Viminal and Palatine into a single city with Romulus and Titus Tatius ruling as joint kings over the considerably enlarged community. The battleground of the valley now became the Forum Romanum (or Roman Forum) – the place, adjacent to the *comitium*, where the former enemies now met to sell and obtain goods and services.

Sabine names were added to the list of those men who were heads of their households – the *patres*, or fathers – and the families descended from those on this roll became the 'patricians' who formed the original aristocratic class of Roman society (see p. 185). As Dionysius remarks, 'They were called patricians because only these men could point out their fathers – all the rest were fugitives and unable to name a free man as their parent' (*Roman Antiquities* 2.8.3).

Titus Tatius was co-ruler for six years. At the end of this time some young Sabines raided the territory of Lavinium, leading to an outraged delegation of Lavinian ambassadors coming to Rome in protest. Lavinium was directly linked to Romulus by family ties, so Romulus wanted the raiders immediately handed over to face justice. He was stymied by Titus Tatius, who as Sabine king had jurisdiction – and Tatius happened to be a close friend of the fathers of some of the miscreants. To compound the felony, as the disappointed ambassadors were making their way back to Lavinium the young Sabines fell upon them and murdered several of the delegation.

Tatius claimed that he had no part in these murders, which were particularly egregious killings as the person of an ambassador was meant to be sacred. Nevertheless, the Sabine king was distinctly lackadaisical in seeking out the perpetrators and shielded them from justice when Romulus eventually tracked them down. Under the circumstances Tatius was probably unwise to go to Lavinium for a sacrifice celebrated by Latins and Sabines alike. He was attacked by the outraged populace and killed with the knives used to slay the sacrificial victims. Romulus was escorted from the city 'with praise for his role in events' (says Plutarch in *Life of Romulus* 23.2) and he thereafter refused to take any action against Lavinium, claiming that the city's people had committed 'murder for murder'.

At this point it is easy to forget that the narrative is legend rather than history. By and large the Romans were remarkably grounded when describing the later parts of the reign of Romulus. The gods politely refrain from intervening in human affairs. Nymphs, monsters and other supernatural creatures fail to make an appearance. There are no bizarre omens or uncannily accurate prophesies. For the most part Romulus behaves almost as a historical ruler, apart from the sort of personal performance on the battlefield that one might expect of a son of Mars.

The Hut of Romulus

The surprisingly prosaic description of Romulus the king has led to some speculation as to whether Romulus was a real person about whom some literally incredible legends had grown. After all, today one can visit the homes of George Washington, Winston Churchill, Charles Dickens and Handel, all preserved as they were when their famous occupants dwelled there. The Romans did the same thing with what they maintained was the house of Romulus, which they carefully preserved on the Palatine. The Romans rather liked to use this crude hut, located as it was beside several splendid imperial palaces, as a visual demonstration of how far their city had come over the centuries.

With the story of Romulus and Remus the Romans appear to have been almost deliberately blending the sublime with the sordid, so it is unsurprising that they kept up this approach right to the very end. As the years went by Romulus became less a man of the people and more of an autocratic ruler. Some writers, such as Plutarch, maintain that success had gone to his head. 'Like many men – well in fact like almost everybody whom good luck has elevated through fortuitous events – the power and position he had gained encouraged him to become more arrogant in his manner' (*Life of Romulus* 26.1).

After a successful war with Veii – the city which was to become Rome's arch-enemy in later years – Romulus arbitrarily divided up the captured lands among his followers without consulting his councillors, let alone the populace in general. This was a serious breach of conduct, at least among later Romans.

IV

Every Roman was expected to call a *concilium* – a meeting of trusted advisors – before making a major decision, whether he be a farmer deciding to sell one of his plough oxen or a king deciding what to do with captured territory.

It is believed that the advisors who were summoned to advise the king were the senior heads of households and for this reason were called 'senators'. ('Senator' and 'senior' have the same linguistic root.) Yet with Romulus becoming more autocratic, the senators complained that the only advantage of their status was that they discovered what Romulus had decided before the news reached the general population. They tended to mutter this only among themselves, however, as Romulus had surrounded himself with a bodyguard of violent young men who were quick to take action if they felt their leader was being disrespected.

About this time Numitor, king of Alba Longa, died. The throne went to his eldest surviving son, who happened to be Romulus. Romulus had his hands full ruling over the less-than-ideal citizen body of Rome and could certainly not become a part-time ruler while he also took over the running of Alba Longa. Nor was he prepared to cede so powerful a position to another. In the end he opted to give Alba a sort of temporary king from among his favourites at court, that king being replaced at the end of each year.

The Consuls

This rotating kingship imposed by Romulus on Alba Longa proved surprisingly successful. The Romans took note, and many years later when they had rebelled and thrown out their king they decided not to replace him. Instead they remembered the example of Romulus in Alba and decided that appointing someone with near-monarchical powers was not a bad idea – provided that the person in question was removed from office on an annual basis. Just to make sure that this temporary king did not get ideas, they yoked him to a colleague as one yokes two oxen to a plough, and each of these *consules* (or 'co-ploughers') had the power to veto the actions of the other.

At this point Romulus had reached his fifty-fifth birthday. Soon thereafter he ceased to be king of Rome. He neither abdicated nor died on the job. Instead he simply vanished. This disappearance was all the more remarkable because it happened in full public view while Romulus was reviewing the army on the Campus Martius. Livy records this marvel in *From the Founding of the City* (1.16.1–2):

> Suddenly a violent thunderstorm brewed up with the cloud so low and dense that Romulus was lost to the sight of those assembled there. He was never seen again, for when the fearsome storm was replaced with calm and bright sunshine, his throne was seen to be empty. Under the circumstances the bewildered populace believed the testimony of the senators. They had been standing next to the king and reported that a sudden tornado had snatched Romulus away to the heavens.

Even at the time, Plutarch assures us, there were those who reckoned the senators were peddling 'a very silly story'.

Fortunately an Alban man called Proculus Julius came forward with remarkable corroborative testimony, which he swore to be true by all that was holy. That is, he had been going peacefully down the road when he was met by a man in shining armour whom he immediately recognized as the transfigured body of his friend Romulus. Asked why he had so suddenly quit as king of Rome, Romulus replied:

> 'Proculus, the gods from whom I am descended decided that I should only briefly live among men. After founding a city which fate shall make glorious with the greatest empire on earth I am now to return to the heavens. Farewell, and tell the Romans that if they can add self-control to their bravery no race shall surpass them in power. I shall be guarding the fortunes of the city as the God Quirinus'.

> (PLUTARCH, *Life of Romulus* 28.2)

Apparently the Romans of the time swallowed this story whole, though Plutarch was more sceptical: 'Many such improbable fables are written', he remarks after listing Greek tales in which a body has inexplicably vanished. He and Livy seem more inclined to the more sordid version of the legend which both say circulated alongside the official version of the lost king's apotheosis.

In this altogether less mystical version, the storm did indeed happen and the low cloud obscured Romulus from view. Realizing this presented a golden opportunity to be rid of an increasingly dictatorial and arbitrary ruler, the senators fell upon Romulus, killed him and literally tore him apart. Then when the clouds cleared they told their tale of the divine

whirlwind while each held a small portion of the late king concealed beneath his toga.

To show they had harboured nothing but goodwill toward Romulus the senate hurried to give concrete expression to the account of Proculus Julius. They immediately set about building their new god Quirinus a temple on one of the seven hills – a hill which they renamed the Quirinal in his honour.

As a footnote to this tale, the Proculus Julius who saw this manifestation of the divine Romulus marks the reappearance of the Julian family who were to become so prominent in the later years of the Republic. This appearance was necessary, as otherwise the line of Aeneas would have ended with Romulus and the Caesars would not have been able to make their claim of descent from the goddess Venus.

V

THREE SABINES AND A CORINTHIAN KING

From Romulus to Rome's last monarch, Tarquinius Superbus (often called Tarquin the Proud), Rome had seven kings. This is a number which should immediately raise suspicions, because, as with the seven hills of Rome, the seven wonders of the ancient world and the seven sages, it is likely that later Romans first decided on the special number seven and then recruited the kings they needed to fill that quota. If, on the other hand, all seven kings were indeed historical figures, it may be that the Romans reached the required number of seven by dropping Titus Tatius from the list rather than by adding imaginary persons.

Legend says that the second king of Rome was Numa Pompilius. By this account, whether or not the senators had indeed assassinated Romulus they were by no means eager to have him replaced by another king. Instead they adopted the rotating kingship which had worked so well in Alba Longa. This did not sit well with the common people of Rome, who felt that a monarch was needed to defend their interests against an aristocracy that might well become overbearing.

If Rome were to have a king, the Sabines reckoned that the new ruler should be one of their own, especially as Romulus had been sole ruler since the untimely death of Titus Tatius. The Romans naturally disagreed, feeling that the next king of Rome should be a Roman. The result was one of those compromises that later generations of Romans regarded as a demonstration that their concept of governance was flexible enough to adapt to new challenges. In this case the Sabines agreed that they would nominate a Roman for the throne. The

Romans would choose a Sabine and collectively they would vote to decide which of the two candidates should be the next ruler of the nascent city.

NUMA POMPILIUS

It is not known whom the Sabines chose, because the Roman alternative was regarded as overwhelmingly the best option. There was an element of dynastic choice here because, while Romulus had died childless, Titus Tatius had sired a daughter and she had married a well-respected man called Numa. Also, with unexpected (and deeply suspicious) felicity, Numa just happened to have been born in the city of Cures on 21 April 753 BC – the very day when Romulus was founding his new city some 42 kilometres (26 miles) away.

The city of Cures did exist, and still does in ruins on a hill-side near the town of Talocci in the district of Fara in Sabina. Archaeological excavations have shown that the site was inhabited since at least the ninth century BC, so it is highly probable that the city was indeed Sabine when Numa was born there.

Also on matters of chronology this seems a good moment to concur with those Roman writers, including Plutarch and Dionysius of Halicarnassus, who disagree with the enduring myth that Numa and the Greek mathematician and philosopher Pythagoras were friends and contemporaries. As Dionysius points out, Pythagoras lived in the city of Croton four generations later, and when Numa came to the throne Croton had not yet been founded. (Which suggests that the early Italians kept careful track of city foundation dates.)

Numa was, at the time, a widower because Tatia, his wife, had recently died and he was now living a quiet and reclusive life. When ambassadors came to offer him sovereignty in Rome, Numa firmly rejected the proposition. Human nature being as it is, as soon as Numa refused to be king even those Romans who had originally objected to him now became eager for him to take the position. It took relentless diplomatic pressure before Numa finally bowed to popular demand and agreed to ascend the throne.

Partly due to the exertions of Romulus, Rome had now achieved local dominance and there were no serious wars for the next generation. This left Numa plenty of time to tidy up the laws and customs of the city, which, having a population formed from the leftovers of Italy, had a hotch-potch of different traditions and legal practices. It helped that Numa preferred diplomacy and alliances to warfare. One of his alleged maxims was 'Don't poke a fire with a sword'.

Plutarch (*Life of Numa* 18.3) argues that Numa rearranged the months. He moved March from its position as the first month of the year, so as to give less prominence to the god Mars after whom the month was named. March was now preceded by January – named after Janus, the god of beginnings – and February, which had been the twelfth and final month and named after Februa, the festival of purification and fasting. (The latter made a virtue of necessity, as this was the hungry month before the harvest of the winter wheat.) This change left the later months of the year out of kilter with their names – something which, with further distortions in the first century, has endured to the present day. *Septem, octo, novem* and *decem* are seven, eight, nine and ten in Latin, but September is now the ninth month and so on to December, the twelfth month.

As to Numa himself, if the man ever existed as a genuine individual then that person has been buried in a mass of legend. Many ancient cities had a lawgiver – Solon of Athens, Lycurgus of Sparta and Minos of Crete being among many examples. These were the people to whom the laws of the city were ascribed, and respect for the ancient lawgiver was often reinforced with a religious connection – for example, Lycurgus is said to have made regular trips to Delphi to be advised by Apollo. So it was with Numa.

Almost any tradition or law of uncertain date was ascribed to his reign. For example the office of Pontifex Maximus was a particularly Roman institution of uncertain origin. Numa was duly believed to have instituted the office. Indeed, once the kingship had been abolished and Rome became a Republic, the Pontifex Maximus moved into the royal house (the Regia) which Numa is said to have built next to the Shrine of Vesta in the Forum – it was also believed that this ancient shrine had been built by Numa. In this way Numa ceased to be a person and became a handy repository for Rome's oldest laws and customs. Any tradition of uncertain origin was attributed to him, and even by the Late Republic it was impossible to distinguish the 'real' Numa from his legend.

According to the tradition linking lawgivers with the gods, Numa would need divine assistance and advice in organizing the city's internal affairs. Livy assures us that Numa arranged for that to happen:

> After he had sealed alliances with neighbouring states, [Rome was at peace and] Numa was able to close the Temple of Janus ... his concern was that the removal

of external threats and the need for military discipline would cause the populace to become idle and decadent. He therefore decided to exchange fear of an enemy with fear of the gods as this would have the most powerful effect upon an uncultured, and indeed in those days, barbarous people.

For this to impress anyone, he needed to maintain that divine wisdom underlay his plans. Therefore he claimed that he had long discussions every night with the nymph Egeria and the rituals and priesthoods that he instituted were by her counsel.

(From the Founding of the City 1.19.4–5)

Livy's fellow historian Dionysius of Halicarnassus reports that even Numa's contemporaries were sceptical of these divine discourses, and the tradition became no more convincing as time passed:

Those who want to strip fables from history consider the story about Egeria as being invented by Numa. The point being that if the people feared the gods and believed that the laws he had enacted came from the gods, they would more willingly listen to him and accept what he proposed.

(Roman Antiquities 2.61.1)

It is disputed whether Numa had any children other than a daughter called (inevitably) Pompilia. All Roman women were named after the *gentilicium* (family name) of their father; so the daughter of Numa Pompilius was called Pompilia just as a daughter of the Julian line was Julia, a Claudian daughter,

Claudia, and so on. Names were very important. In later years some aristocrats were accused of leaning on genealogists to give their families a venerable and ancient origin – a case of posterity begetting ancestors rather than the other way around. Thus the noble family of the Calpurnii, for example, came up with an ancestor called Calpus, whom they insisted was a previously unknown son of Numa.

The Ancile

Those who remained dubious of Numa's divine connections may have been reassured by a shield that dropped into the city from the heavens. At the same time a voice was heard to proclaim that Rome would rule the world so long as this item was preserved. This shield, which was known as the *ancile*, was of the ancient wasp-waisted design sometimes called the 'Mycenaean figure eight'. The shape is known because the shield was preserved into historical times, kept by the *collegium* of priests called the Salii, and is present in depictions of the priests in procession.

This shield thus served Rome as a symbol of divine protection, just as the already-ancient Palladium had served Troy. Indeed, the arrival of the shield coincided with the end of a plague which had been killing the people of the city. Numa was well aware that the Palladium had secured the safety of Troy only until it was stolen by Odysseus. Accordingly he took precautions that the same should not happen to his own city's magical protector. On the basis that it was a lot harder to steal a dozen objects than a single

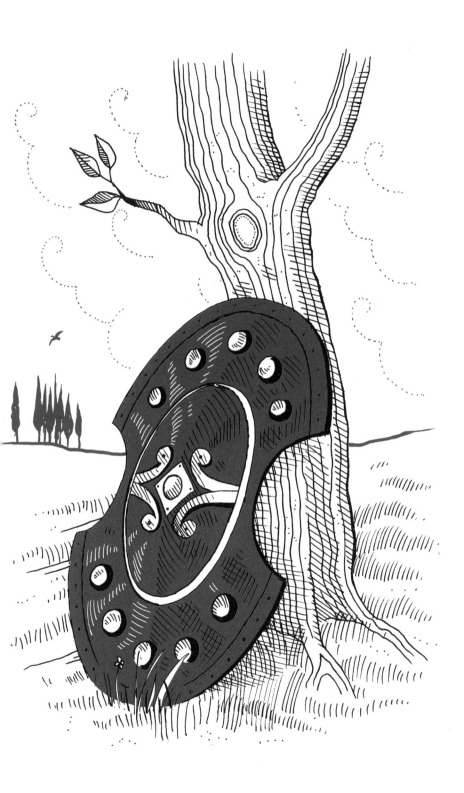

item, Numa commissioned a master-craftsman called Mamurius to make eleven replicas of the shield, which Mamurius did – so exactly that posterity never knew which was the original.

TULLUS HOSTILIUS

Another such clan – with a much better claim – were the Marcii, allegedly descended from one of the ambassadors who had originally urged Numa to take the throne. This man married Pompilia and they had a son called Numa Marcius. When Numa eventually died after a forty-three year reign (in his eighties, peacefully from old age) this son made a bid to become the next king of Rome. However, neither senate nor people were yet ready for a dynastic kingship and the throne went to another Sabine, Tullus Hostilius, the grandson of a hero who had died in the war against Romulus.

There was a degree of sentiment among Rome's neighbours that the city had gone soft during the long and placid reign of Numa, and some surrounding cities were eager to test the mettle of the new king. Foremost among these were the people of Alba Longa, who chafed at being ruled from a city which their own people had founded. Albans raided Roman lands and retaliatory Roman raids produced a further escalation of hostilities. This ended with the king of Alba breaking the historic tie with Rome and thereafter both cities moved to a war footing.

Usually no ancient Italian city had much hesitation in going to war, but this time there were two major issues to be considered. Firstly, Romans and Albans had a long mutual history and deep ties of commerce and intermarriage, so any conflict would be akin to a civil war. Secondly, the Etruscan neighbours of both Rome and Alba Longa were watching with predatory interest, hoping for a conflict which would weaken both sides to the extent that the Etruscans could swoop in and conquer winner and loser alike. The solution was not to throw the entire armies of both sides into a bloody conflict, but to find champions to fight in their stead.

THE BATTLE OF THE CHAMPIONS AND THE END OF ALBA LONGA

As it happened, each army had a set of triplets within its ranks. The Romans had the Horatian triplets and the Albans three Curiatii. The six knew each other well – in fact Horatia, the sister of the three Horatii, was betrothed to one of the Curiatii. Despite this potential kinship it was agreed that the triplets would slug it out in a three-on-three combat to the death and the winners would determine which city had mastery over the other. Though he had more to lose, Tullus agreed to these terms because he was confident that his Horatii were the superior fighters.

It came as something of a shock, therefore, when the first clash of arms ended with all three Curiatii wounded with various degrees of severity, but two of the three Horatii dead on the ground. The odds were now three to one. The surviving Horatius was evidently a strategic thinker – which is possibly why he was unwounded in the first place. He fled – not to escape but to put the fight on his own terms. He reasoned that with each of his opponents wounded he could win if he fought them singly. Because of their different wounds the Curiatii

who gave chase ended up strung out across the field of combat. The surviving Horatius turned on the leader, slew him, moved briskly on to the second in line, and having dispatched him moved on to do the same with the third. Rome had won.

Writing some six centuries later, the historian Livy informs us (in *From the Founding of the City* 1.25.13): 'Each was buried where he fell. Their tombs are there still. The two Romans are close together towards Alba, the three Albans nearer Rome and each separate from the other, just where each fight took place.'

The surviving Horatius returned to Rome accompanied by a rejoicing populace. As he entered Rome he discovered that joy was not universal. His sister Horatia was hysterical with grief and furious with Horatius for killing her beloved Curiatius. Horatius, himself in the grip of heightened emotion, responded by running his sister through with his sword. Even in those days the Romans were sticklers for the law. Murder was murder so, saviour of the state or no, Horatius was put on trial – and sentenced to death. Meanwhile a sixth tomb – also extant in Livy's day – was built near the Capuan Gate on the spot where Horatia had been slain.

As was his right in law, Horatius appealed to the people. The Romans were always deeply reluctant to put their own citizens to death, and a convoluted process of appeal and legalistic wrangling inevitably followed a death sentence (which was often commuted to exile). Horatius's second tribunal required the entire Roman people to assemble to give their collective judgment. The most powerful speaker at Horatius's trial was the father of the accused, who asked whether, having given the lives of two sons for Rome, he was to lose another. He claimed that his daughter had been justly slain and were it otherwise he himself would have killed his son (as Roman law allowed). Horatius was duly acquitted, but this was not the end of the matter.

In the end, the Battle of the Champions did no more than restore an unsatisfactory status quo. This was the time for Tullus to rebuild Rome's relationship with Alba Longa from a position of strength – an opportunity he squandered. Instead he moved on immediately to deal with another restive people, the citizens of nearby Fidenae. This city had been conquered by Romulus, but now thanks to some subversive diplomacy from Rome's rival, the Etruscan city of Veii, the city had thrown off Roman rule. Tullus aimed for a speedy reconquest.

The Roman army was drawn up in battle array and was preparing to engage with the Fidentines when the Alban contingent suddenly withdrew, exposing the Roman flank. The Romans won anyway, but the battle was a close-run thing and a furious Tullus took immediate action against the Albans. The Alban king was literally torn apart by being tied between chariots driven in different directions. The Alban army was disarmed.

Thereafter Roman soldiers came to Alba Longa to order the citizenry to pack up their homes and move to Rome forthwith. When the populace had left, 'The Romans flattened every building, public and private, in the entire city. After a short time they had eradicated the legacy of the four hundred years of Alba's existence' (Livy, *From the Founding of the City* 1.29.6). To accommodate this sudden explosion of the population of the city of Rome, the Caelian hill was brought within the city limits.

Although Tullus had ordered that the temples of Alba Longa be spared demolition, evidently the destruction of the ancestral home of the Romans had displeased the gods, for

Rome was smitten with a plague. Faced with an enemy he could not conquer with the sword, Tullus turned to the techniques of his predecessor Numa and sought to placate the gods through magical ritual. In the privacy of his home Tullus attempted 'sacrifices of a secret and solemn nature' (says Livy). However experienced he was in warfare, Tullus was untrained in the arcane arts, so his magical experiments were the equivalent of a modern amateur defusing a large bomb with the help of a handbook.

During the course of the ritual Tullus was apparently killed by a sudden thunderbolt. 'Apparently' because it proved impossible to sift his ashes from those of his house, which was obliterated at the same time. In any case this event explosively marked the end of Tullus's thirty-two-year reign and also, as it happened, the end of the plague.

ANCUS MARCIUS

The Roman people assembled to choose their new king and decided that, after all, electing the family of Numa was not a bad idea. Numa's grandson Ancus Marcius duly became the fourth king of Rome, just over a century from the time the city had been founded by Romulus. By all accounts (basically those of Livy and Dionysius) Marcius was a competent ruler. He combined the religious expertise of Numa with the military ability of Tullus and extended Roman rule to include the port of Ostia.

Rome's population was Latin and Sabine, but not all Latins and Sabines were Romans. Those outside Rome's citizen body were both jealous and fearful of Rome's growing power and combined to restrain it. Their success – or rather lack of it – can be seen in the further expansion of the city of Rome. Following the example of his predecessors, Marcius transferred captured peoples to his city and this led to the settlement of the Transtiberim district on the slopes of the Janiculum. (This ridge on the west bank of the Tiber was so named because these slopes were the fields of Janus when that god ruled the area in the primordial age.) Being across the Tiber, the Transtiberim district made necessary the construction of Rome's first bridge. This was the Sublician Bridge, which has since been rebuilt numerous times after fires, floods and wars. The current incarnation is an elegant two-arched structure rebuilt completely in 1918.

The Mamertine Prison

Another relic of the reign of Ancus Marcius is the Mamertine prison, which is arguably the oldest building in twenty-first-century Rome. Built on the slopes of the Capitoline hill, the prison was originally a cistern to hold water from the spring (*tullius* in Latin) which gave the edifice its ancient name of the Tullianum. (The name the 'Mamertine prison' comes from the medieval era, and probably refers to the shrine to the god Mars which the Romans later built nearby.)

The Romans worked out that a deep bowl into which people had to be lowered made for a remarkably escape-proof place to keep prisoners. The Tullianum was not very large because the Romans did not believe in imprisonment as a form of punishment. Those occupying the cistern did so for the very brief period between capture, trial and subsequent execution. Famous occupants of the Tullianum included the Numidian King Jugurtha, the Gallic King Vercingetorix, the conspirators in the failed Catiline plot to overthrow the government of Rome in the first century BC, and St Peter. Catholic authorities rather irritably dismiss the story that the spring at the base of the building came miraculously into being to allow St Peter to baptise the other prisoners.

TARQUINIUS PRISCUS (TARQUIN THE ELDER)

Rome's fifth king is an interesting character, not least because he is named after an Etruscan city. This is the city of Tarquinia, which today lies 100 kilometres (62 miles) down the E80 motorway from Rome. Three thousand years ago the Etruscans called their city Tarchna. Even then this city was one of the major settlements in the region. Archaeological evidence has revealed that the Etruscans as a whole traded extensively with the Greeks and shared much of a common culture. (Interestingly the Etruscan alphabet is derived from the Greek and contains several antique letters which were dropped from the classical Greek version of the language.)

Therefore, it is not improbable that Tarchna/Tarquinia provided a hospitable shelter for a Greek exile called Demaratus, who fled to that city after getting into political trouble in his native Corinth. This is what the legend relates, and it is by no means the only case of what anthropologists call 'horizontal mobility' in the Archaic era (the period between roughly 700 and 500 BC – though some places stayed archaic longer than others). Horizontal mobility is when a person from one city

– or culture – moves to another without any loss of status. Thus a craftsman from Athens could move to Rome and set up shop there, or an aristocrat from Corinth could move to Etruria and keep his noble status. Among the politically engaged nobility of the Mediterranean world exile was always a threat, and those granting asylum to people expelled from their native land were keenly aware that shifting political fortunes might later mean that the favour needed to be returned.

The Romans later credited Demaratus with an outsize effect upon Etruscan culture. ('The Etruscans learned their letters from the Corinthian Demaratus' says Tacitus in *Annals* 11.14.) According to legend, Demaratus imported a large number of craftsmen from his home town and set about making a second fortune – he took the first one with him when he left Corinth – by flooding Etruria with Greek pottery. (As it happens, archaeologists in Tuscany have unearthed a great deal of Corinthian pottery dated to this period.) Demaratus married an Etruscan noblewoman and passes peacefully from the record after bequeathing two sons to posterity.

One of these sons died soon after his marriage, but the other (who was called 'Lucius', meaning that he had been born at the first light of day) found life in Tarchna frustrating. His ancestry and wealth caused him to believe that he should rank highly in the councils of his adoptive city. However, even his marriage to Tanaquil, a lady of a prestigious family, did not prevent the natives from seeing him as a foreigner and excluding him from the innermost circle of government. In the end it was the wife of Lucius who came up with the solution – they should leave town and head for Rome, a growing city where for men with talent and wealth, the sky was the limit.

Destiny Foretold

Livy vividly describes a favourable omen that Lucius received on the way to Rome (*From the Founding of the City* 1.34.7–9):

> So, they assembled their possessions and set out for Rome. They had reached the Janiculum and were sitting in their travelling carriage* when an eagle glided down and seized the cap which he [Lucius] was wearing, after which it noisily flapped off to its original height. Then, as if ordered by the gods to do so, it stooped once more, neatly replaced the cap upon his head and flew off.
>
> As were many Etruscans, Tanaquil was skilled in the interpretation of divine events and they say that she joyfully accepted the promise of this auspicious event. She embraced her husband and told him he would achieve great things. This was foretold by the species of the bird, the quarter of the sky from which the bird had appeared, the god of whom that bird was the totemic animal [Jupiter] and that highest part of the man [the head] which had been affected.

* Livy's mention of the travelling carriage (*carpentum*) is interesting because this form of transport, favoured by travelling aristocrats, had a curved wooden roof. One can only assume that Tarquin was sitting outside at the dashboard, which makes all the more extraordinary the effort of the eagle to seize and replace the cap. (Dashboards were originally to protect people from dirt thrown up – 'dashed' – by the horses hooves.)

Given that Lucius had wealth and abundant foreign connections, it comes as no surprise that he was immediately accepted in Rome. Here he acquired the position he had desired in Tarquinia – a seat at the innermost councils of the king. In fact, so trusted was he that the king made Lucius the guardian of his sons. This was particularly important because, after ruling for twenty-four years, Ancus Marcius was in failing health. Indeed, it soon became apparent to Lucius (who by now had adopted Tarquinius as a surname after his city of origin) that the king was on the brink of death. Through his position as royal advisor and guardian, Lucius Tarquinius managed to hide from the king's sons the parlous state of their father's health. When it was certain that Marcius would expire within the next day or so, Tarquinius contrived an excuse to send the sons out of Rome.

Tarquinius then announced the death of the king to the popular assembly, and at the same time successfully made his case for being named as Marcius's successor. The king's sons would have welcomed the chance to present themselves as candidates, but they were unfortunately out of town. This cynical ruse by Tarquinius was something that the sons of Marcius neither forgot nor forgave.

As often happened after a change of ruler in Rome, the neighbours immediately tested the new king's military ability. King Tarquinius (widely known to classicists as Tarquinius Priscus, or in translation as 'Tarquin the Elder') was forced to fight those Latins who lived outside Rome and were fearful of being absorbed by the growing monster by the Tiber. When Tarquinius proved highly competent at rebuffing their pre-emptive attack, the Latins called in the Sabines to help. The

Sabines had the same motivation as the Latins and once they were fully involved in war with Rome the Etruscans scented vulnerability and joined in.

The Legend of the Whetstone

Tarquinius found himself short of manpower and wanted to expand the cavalry by adding another unit to the 'tribes' into which the Romans were divided for military purposes. This led to a spat with the chief diviner of the day, a man called Accius Naevius. Naevius insisted that he should take the auguries before any action was taken. Refusing to be second-guessed by a priest, Tarquin said he would consent to that – but only if the auguries first decided whether what he was now thinking was possible.

Naevius accordingly took the auguries and determined that whatever Tarquinius had in mind was indeed possible. Tarquinius then sprang his trap and passed a razor to Naevius. 'I was thinking that you could slice that whetstone over there in two with this', he explained.

Unperturbed by the apparent impossibility of the challenge, Naevius took the razor and cut through the whetstone as though it were a freshly baked cake. Livy assures us that thereafter the miraculous whetstone was preserved in the Roman Forum as a reminder to posterity never to underestimate the power of augury.

The talent for original thinking that had brought Tarquinius to the throne also enabled his most spectacular victory over

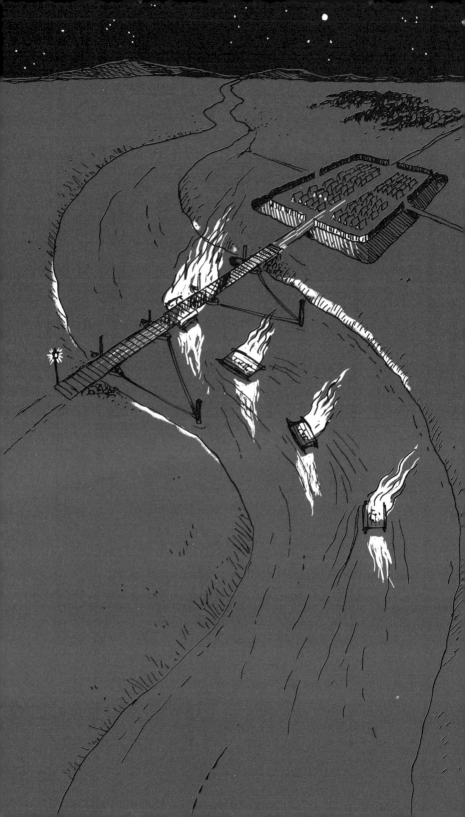

the Sabines. Their army had crossed a river in large numbers and set up a camp on the Roman bank, which they supplied by means of a bridge that they had built over the river. Tarquinius prepared flaming rafts and sent them downriver to burn the bridge, creating a fire which also engulfed the Sabine encampment. At the same moment the Romans launched a ferocious attack. The result was a comprehensive victory, which largely knocked the Sabines out of the war. Subsequently Tarquinius celebrated the first of the very many Roman triumphs which were to take place over subsequent centuries.

Despite his successful generalship, Tarquinius reckoned Rome would only be safe if the walls were expanded to contain the now much larger city. Also he felt it would be wise to set up a temple of Jupiter on the Mount of Saturn (later to be called the Capitoline hill). He started making plans for this, even as he turned the flat space below into the chariot-racing track of the Circus Maximus. Chariots had been raced there since the time of Romulus, but later generations credited Tarquinius with draining the marsh to make racing possible all year round. Tarquinius was also said to have added formal turning points for the chariots and seating for the spectators.

He also adopted an heir – and this probably led to his death. The sons of Ancus Marcius had always reckoned that Tarquinius was a usurper, but up to this point they had been biding their time. The king was not getting any younger and there was a good chance that one of them would be elected his successor. Except now Tarquinius and Tanaquil had adopted a youth called Servius Tullius and were publicly grooming him to become the next king of Rome.

V

Accordingly the sons of Marcius devised a plot to remove the king before he could formally announce Tullius as his heir. Two shepherds staged a very public altercation outside the palace. Tarquinius overheard the quarrel and invited the two men within so that he might judge their case. In fact, the 'shepherds' were assassins recruited by the sons of Marcius. As soon as Tarquinius turned his attention to one 'shepherd' the other crept up behind him and killed him with a blow to the head. Thus Tarquinius perished in the thirty-eighth year of his reign – leaving the question of the succession wide open.

VI

THE
SLAVE
AND
THE
TYRANT

It was a point of pride with the Romans of the Late Republic that their city was open to men of talent, whosoever they were, and howsoever they had arrived in Rome. As an example from their own time they might mention one Publius Ventidius, who participated in two Roman triumphs. In the first Ventidius was but a boy, a captive paraded through Rome in the 89 BC triumph of Pompey Strabo (the father of Pompey the Great) who had captured his native city.

Ventidius was later freed and joined the Roman army, where he became a favourite of Julius Caesar. Later he commanded Roman forces in the east and won an overwhelming victory over Parthian invaders. This resulted in the second appearance of Ventidius in a Roman triumph – this time honoured as the *triumphator* – the victorious general.

To show that their city had always been a haven for the upwardly mobile, the Romans could point to the sixth king of Rome, Servius Tullius, whose reign is dated from 578–535 BC. Like Ventidius, Servius came to Rome as a captive. This led later etymologists to link the name Servius with *servus* (slave). This word origin is probably false, or noble families such as the Servii Sulpicii – who produced a Roman emperor in AD 68/69 – would not have used it so proudly.

While the Romans liked their legends to be specific, the legends were sometimes specific about points that contradicted each other. So we are told that Servius was definitely the son of a nobleman who perished when his native city of Corniculum was captured by Tarquinius, and also that he was the son of a slave woman from Tarchna (Tarquinia). None other than the emperor Claudius reckoned that, in fact, Servius had originally been an Etruscan soldier called Mastarna (Tacitus, *Annals* 11.24).

By Ovid's more sensational account, Servius was conceived by divine power while his mother was already a slave in Rome:

> The father of Servius was Vulcan, and his mother,
>   the beauteous Ocresia of Corniculum.
> It happened that after properly performing the sacred
>   rituals by the garlanded hearth,
> Tanaquil [the wife of Tarquinius] ordered her to pour
>   wine as a libation.
> Immediately a penis appeared in the ashes – not just
>   a shape but the real thing.
> As commanded the captive girl squats over the hearth
>   and receives the divine seed
> And so was conceived Servius.
>
> (*Fasti* 6.627ff)

To add to the dramatic circumstances of Servius's origins comes a further legend. Everyone is at least agreed that, however Servius came to be in Rome, he definitely ended up in the household of the king. There, while he was sleeping, an extraordinary corona of fire was seen to surround his head. At once those who witnessed the phenomenon rushed off to call Tanaquil, since the king's wife was an acknowledged expert in matters oracular.

By some accounts no one knew of the divine origins of Servius but Tanaquil, for she and Servius's mother had (conveniently) agreed to keep this a secret. Tanaquil saw this latest revelation as further proof of the divine destiny of Servius and proclaimed that the nimbus of fire about his head meant that

the gods had singled the lad out for great things. Thereafter, Tanaquil and Tarquinius began treating Servius as their adopted son and heir.

As already noted, the elevation of Servius did not sit well with the sons of Marcius. They had Tarquinius assassinated, but their plan to pre-empt Servius's accession to the abruptly vacant throne failed because Tanaquil was every bit as astute a politician as her late husband. Had she announced immediately that he was dead, a power vacuum would have resulted – with several candidates eager to fill the vacant space. So instead Tanaquil informed the populace that Tarquinius, though severely injured, had survived. Until he could resume his regular duties, Servius would stand in for the king.

Servius and Tanaquil kept up this pretence for several days until the reins of power were firmly in their grip. Then they announced that, sadly, Tarquinius had died of his injuries – but those behind the assassination would be hunted down. The sons of Marcius took the hint and fled into exile, leaving Servius Tullius undisputed master of Rome.

SERVIUS THE KING

Cicero, in his work *On the Republic* (2.37), has one of his characters remark: 'It is perfectly evident that every king built numerous beneficial institutions. But [Servius], in my opinion, knew better than any of the others how a state should be governed.'

Just as the Romans used Numa as a legendary depository of any long-established religious ritual or laws, so Servius became the legendary founder of Republican institutions when the true origin of these institutions had vanished into the mists of time. By this account, one of the first things that Servius did was to expand the voting rights of the plebeians. This may reflect a real (but more drawn-out) struggle between aristocrats and commoners in the fledgling Roman state; or it may indeed be true that an autocrat (possibly named Servius Tullius) decided to extend the franchise as a way to outflank an aristocracy suspicious of his ignoble upbringing.

As part of this reform Servius largely replaced the *comitia curiata* with the *comitia centuriata*. Both were formal gatherings convoked by a magistrate to vote on important matters, but the older assembly had been dominated by Rome's great families. The replacement, though by no means totally democratic, was at least a substantial step in that direction. Voting power now depended on what each citizen could bring to war. Those who came equipped with armour and a warhorse had more voting power than those who came only with a set of armour and weapons, and these in turn outranked skirmishers, who were above the very poor whose only contribution to a battle was to hang around the fringes throwing rocks.

Servius also expanded the city of Rome – yet again – and made his home on the Esquiline to encourage settlement on that unpopular hill. (There was an ancient graveyard near the Esquiline summit and even in the imperial period unburied corpses were dumped on the hillside.)

Servius is also credited with freeing many of the plebeians from debt-bondage. This happened when peasant farmers (as were most Romans of this period) got into trouble and had to borrow to get the seed for the next year's harvest into the ground. If that harvest failed, then the borrower had basically to sell himself to his creditor.

The Servian Wall

As the city again expanded, it again needed a new defensive wall. We know a lot about this wall, because some of it is still standing in modern Rome. The wall was built from tuff – a volcanic material which is soft when excavated, but which hardens to stone on exposure to air. Judging by the modern remains, the wall was some 10 metres (33 feet) high, and according to ancient sources it extended for over 10 kilometres (6 miles) around the city. A ditch increased the height of the outward-facing part of the wall.

For centuries the Servian Wall was Rome's only defensive barrier, being superseded only in the late Empire. There is fierce debate as to when this wall was actually built, with some claiming it dates to the early Roman Republic and literalists claiming that sources correctly state that the wall was built in the regal period. Certainly much of the wall can be dated to the Republic, but then, rebuilding was necessary on later occasions. Those wishing to see the wall for themselves can enjoy a hamburger while viewing one of the best-preserved parts of the structure. This is by the Termini railway station and it runs right through a nearby fast-food joint.

The exact medium of exchange for these debts is another hotly disputed question. The Romans themselves recorded that Servius made paying off debts easier by producing the first minted coinage in the city. This is possible but unlikely. The first coins had been minted in Lydia in Anatolia almost a century beforehand, so there was certainly time for the idea to have reached Rome. In fact the earliest Italian coins do date from the Servian period in Rome, but these were produced by Greek cities in the Italian south. The earliest truly Roman coins discovered date to two centuries after Servius.

As a means of bringing the plebeians to his cause Servius even freed some men from debt-bondage by personally repaying their debts. He also made farmland available for some of the Roman poor. Though he took care to get the common people on his side Servius simultaneously tried to secure his other flank against the restive aristocracy by binding his family closer to that of his predecessor, Lucius Tarquinius.

By some accounts Servius married a daughter of the Tarquin family; by others he married a woman called Gegania – whose patrician family was in later years one of the most ancient and venerable in Rome. Tanaquil is said to have personally woven the bridal dress for his wedding. Six centuries later, the scholar Pliny the Elder reports having seen this garment and the distaff and spindle used in the weaving, for they were preserved for posterity respectively in the Shrine of Fortuna and at the Temple of Sancus (Pliny, *Natural History* 8.74.1). Soon thereafter, Tanaquil adopted the more Roman name of Gaia Caecilia, When she fell ill Servius considered abdicating the throne, but Tanaquil on her deathbed made him swear to soldier on.

Whomever Servius married, she had cause for jealousy, for Servius felt that in order to counter suspicions about the legitimacy of his rule (which suspicions proved ineradicable among the aristocracy) he should take a leaf from the tactics of Numa. Accordingly Servius developed a close relationship with the goddess Fortuna – a relationship which, after the death of his wife, became a 'divine marriage'. Plutarch reports in *De Fortuna Romanorum* (On the fortune of the Romans) 10:

> Servius Tullius was the king who most greatly increased the strength of Rome. He established a well-governed state with orderly elections and military procedure, while he was himself the first Censor who supervised the conduct and decorum of his people. His reputation for courage and wisdom came because he attached himself closely to Fortune – so closely that it was believed she lay with him, entering his rooms through that window which today they call the Porta Fenestella. [This 'Postern Gate' has since vanished and its original location is now unknown.]

Servius had no son, but two daughters (both, thanks to Roman naming convention, called Tullia). These he linked to the family of Tarquinius Priscus by marrying his eldest daughter to one Lucius Tarquin and the other to Lucius's brother Arruns. Both were marriages of opposites. Lucius Tarquin had that disposition which led to him later being called *Superbus* or 'The Proud'. His wife was a placid, gentle type – unlike her younger sister who was hot-headed, ambitious and rather upset about being paired with the mild and retiring Arruns. Since members of extended Roman families met frequently (and still do) it did not take long for Lucius Tarquin and the younger Tullia each to discover in the other a kindred spirit.

When it came to obstacles in the path of their ambition the pair were ruthless to the point of sociopathy. The gentle elder Tullia died suddenly in suspicious circumstances. Then the unassuming Arruns died equally suddenly and inexplicably.

This left both Tarquin and the younger Tullia free to choose another spouse – and naturally they chose each other. On then, to the next stage.

Tarquin began to cultivate the aristocracy, especially senators with ties to his family. He pointed out that, while the senators had previously chosen Rome's kings, Servius had been appointed by popular acclamation and – Tarquin made clear – through the machinations of Tanaquil. And she, as a woman, had no business being in politics in the first place. This was ironic, because (according to Livy) the younger Tullia was up to her neck in politics, acting as a sort of Roman Lady Macbeth to drive her husband to think the unthinkable:

> 'If you don't have the nerve for this, why have you been getting everyone's hopes up? Why do you let people see you as a prince of the royal line? Go back to Tarchna or Corinth – vanish into the mass of common people. You are more like your brother than your father.'

> She goaded him on with taunts like this, for she saw herself as a rival to Tanaquil, who although a foreigner had secured the throne first for her husband ... Yet she, though a princess born, had been unable to secure the crown for another.

> *(From the Founding of the City 1.47.5–6)*

Finally, when Tarquin reckoned that he had mustered enough support, he took himself to the senate while it was meeting and sat in the throne usually occupied by Servius. Tarquin then proceeded to denounce his father-in-law to the stunned assembly, claiming that he, of the line of Tarquinius

(even in ancient times it was disputed whether he was a son or grandson of Tarquinius Priscus) was the true king of Rome. Servius, he claimed, was a usurper who had gained the throne by trickery.

Servius had by then ruled Rome for over forty years. He was elderly and had less patience with diplomacy than before, and senators whose pride he had failed to appease now joined in supporting Tarquin. When Servius was finally appraised of the danger and hurried into the senate house Tarquin picked him up and forcibly threw him out again. As he made his way home Servius was set upon – either by partisans of Tarquin, or more probably by hired thugs – and beaten to death.

Tullia then went on to compound the felony. She had hurried to the senate house to support her husband, but Tarquin was not sure that the violence had ceased and ordered her to return home. On the way Tullia came across the body of her father still lying in the street. When the driver of her carriage attempted to halt the horses, Tullia seized the reins and drove over the corpse. She arrived home splattered with her father's blood. It was not the most auspicious beginning to her husband's reign.

TARQUIN II 'THE PROUD', LAST KING OF ROME

'Even the most competent of kings would have difficulty taking the place of one as capable as Servius', remarks Livy (*From the Founding of the City* 1.48.8). It quickly became clear that Tarquin was not even going to try. Instead he planned to secure his throne by terror and violence. Starting as he meant to go on, Tarquin purged the senate, executing any remaining partisans of the late king, whose body he denied burial.

As many a dictator has done since, Tarquin tried to distract his disaffected populace with military adventures abroad. First he secured an alliance with the other Latin peoples who lived in the region, putting Rome at the head of what has become known as the Latin League. The Latin leader who opposed his takeover of the league was accused of plotting to kill Tarquin. Evidence (carefully planted beforehand) was found in his rooms and the man was duly executed.

With the Latins as allies, Tarquin went on to wage an unnecessary war against a people known as the Volsci. He also captured the city of Gabii by a trick. He had his son Sextus beaten black and blue. Sextus then fled to Gabii, his whole body a testament to his father's mistreatment. When Tarquin sent an envoy demanding the return of Sextus and threatening dire consequences otherwise, the trusting populace welcomed Sextus as an ally. Sextus arranged to put his henchmen in charge of a vital city gate and opened it for his father's troops. Once Tarquin's soldiers were inside, he quickly gained control of the city. (So says Dionysius of Halicarnassus, in *Roman Antiquities* 4.58.1.)

Tall Poppies

Legend has it that when Sextus became ruler of Gabii he sent a messenger to his father to ask for advice as to how he should proceed. However, Tarquin knew better than to give the necessary advice openly because he knew this might later be used against him.

Therefore, the messenger returned in a state of some confusion and informed Sextus that Tarquin had hardly spoken to him other than to order him to come along on a royal stroll. Sextus asked what his father had done while on the walk, and the messenger replied that the king had amused himself by slashing the heads off poppies growing alongside the path. Not every poppy, the messenger amended, but only the tallest ones.

Sextus dismissed the messenger, for he understood the message. Over the following weeks the 'tall poppies' – the leading men of Gabii – were either arrested and executed on trumped-up charges, or driven into exile.

In the modern world 'tall poppy syndrome' has been derived from this tale. Today the term signifies the feeling that those who stand out from the crowd somehow need cutting down to size. Interestingly the same tale appears in the *History* (5.92) of Herodotus, featuring Periander, tyrant of Corinth, though in his case it was the tallest ears of wheat that suffered.

With peace on Rome's borders, Tarquin set about realizing the project of Tarquinius Priscus, who before his death had been planning to build a massive temple to Jupiter atop the Mount of Saturn, which some were now calling the Tarpeian hill and which is today the Capitoline.

There had always been other temples on this hill – it was a long-established religious site – but these had been moved off after a careful process of consulting auguries and through divination. All that is, except the altar of the god Terminus. Though asked through a variety of divinations whether he was prepared to yield his place, the god stubbornly refused to accede. Eventually the soothsayers decided that keeping the altar of Terminus in place was a good omen, for Terminus was the god of boundaries; surely his refusal to be moved meant that the borders of Rome would likewise be secure.

The soothsayers faced a greater challenge with the next omen. When work began on the temple foundations, 'the excavation had reached a substantial depth when the head of a man was discovered. He appeared newly-slain and warm, fresh blood flowed from the severed neck' (Dionysius of Halicarnassus, *Roman Antiquities* 4.59.2). Rather than enquire as to mundane causes (had any of the diggers recently had a terminal quarrel with a fellow worker and swiftly buried the evidence?) Tarquin immediately decided that this was a message from the gods and he immediately suspended work on the building while a convocation of soothsayers pondered what it might mean.

According to Livy the convocation reached a conclusion, while Dionysius believes that the Romans finally had to consult a leading Etruscan soothsayer. In each case the ultimate verdict was the same. The head signified that Rome would become the head of the world. This came as a relief to Tarquin since the omen could have signified much worse. It could have meant, for example, that the king – as head of state – was going to be cut off from the civic body. But given Tarquin's habit of arbitrary executions, the soothsayers wisely chose not to mention this. So Tarquin decided to promote the auspicious discovery of the head (*caput* in Latin) by renaming the hill the Capitoline, and making the planned Temple of Jupiter even more grandiose.

Tarquin had also embarked upon another major construction project – the draining of the marshy Forum by means of a large ditch, which would also act to carry the effluent of the

THE SLAVE AND THE TYRANT

growing city into the Tiber. This latter edifice became the most famous sewer in the world – the Cloaca Maxima. It is still reliably carrying away Roman waste twenty-six hundred years later.

The workforce for these huge undertakings was supplied by the Roman plebs. In Tarquin's reckoning, his diplomacy had brought peace beyond Rome's borders, but that was no reason why the levy should sit idle. So – establishing that same tradition that had Roman legionaries of later eras building roads and bridges – Tarquin told his soldiers to exchange their spears for shovels and get digging. The men did, but they were not very happy about it.

The Cloaca Maxima

The Romans were very proud of their sewer. It even had its own goddess – Venus Cloacina (who for reasons we need not go into here was also the goddess of sex within marriage). Water was kept flowing by channelling streams from the hillside opposite. When the Tiber overflowed and flooded the Forum, the Cloaca Maxima also acted as a giant drain. There is no reason to disbelieve that work started during the period when Rome was still ruled by kings. None of the very ancient buildings in the Forum could have been constructed in a marsh, so draining that marsh by means of the Cloaca Maxima was a necessary prequel.

Tarquin could not be accused of thinking small. Thousands of cubic metres of earth were shifted in the construction and the final sewer was wide enough for loaded wagons (says the geographer Strabo) to pass through. Indeed, at the start of the Empire, when Augustus's henchman Agrippa was planning renovations of the sewer, he first toured the site underground in a boat. Usually the task of sewer maintenance was so unpleasant that the job was given to condemned criminals (Pliny the Younger, *Letters* 10.32).

THE SIBYLLINE BOOKS

That the gods were taking a deep interest in what was still the insignificant little kingdom of Rome was already apparent thanks to the numerous prodigies and divine revelations explaining Rome's future greatness. Nevertheless, the gods clearly felt that more direct guidance was needed if the Romans were to do things by the book. Three books, in fact. These were oracular texts of great antiquity which apparently made their way to Rome from the area of ancient Troy by way of the Greek city of Cumae.

Why books from the other side of the Mediterranean should be particularly relevant to the fate of Rome is uncertain – though the Trojan location does give a certain Roman connection via Aeneas. Today no one knows what was in the books, for they were guarded by close-mouthed priests. In fact one custodian, a certain Marcus Acilius, who allowed part of one text to be copied by people from another city, was put to death by being sewn into a sack and thrown into the Tiber – a punishment usually reserved for parricides (Cassius Dio, *Roman History* 2.11)

Some of the contents of the books were lost to fire in later ages and other texts were destroyed as blasphemous in the Christian era. (They were 'replaced' by the so-called *Sibylline Oracles*, which are a completely different kettle of Judeo-

Christian fish.) However, while they had them the Romans carefully consulted the books whenever there were great disasters, inexplicable phenomena or devastating wars.

How King Tarquin came to possess the books was told almost a millennium later in the notes of one Aulus Gellius (*Attic Nights* 1.19):

> The ancient accounts give us this legend about the Sibylline Books. One day an aged woman whom no one had seen before came to King Tarquin. She brought with her for sale nine books containing prophecies from the Gods. When Tarquin asked how much these books would cost she named an exorbitantly large price.
>
> Believing the woman to be senile the king laughed off the proposed sale, whereupon the woman placed a lighted brazier in front of him and proceeded to burn three of the books. She then offered the remaining books for sale at the same price as before. Tarquin found the idea hilarious and declared that the old woman was undoubtedly insane.
>
> Calmly the woman proceeded to burn another three books, and still asked the same price for the surviving texts. Now Tarquin became intrigued by her confidence and started to consider her price seriously. Finally he purchased the three books for the price originally asked for all nine. Thereafter the woman left the king's presence and was never seen again.
>
> The books were called 'Sibylline' [a sibyl was a wise woman with powers of prophecy] and placed in a

dedicated shrine. Here a select committee consults the books whenever the guidance of the immortal gods is needed for the welfare of Rome.

A Very Exclusive Library

After the expulsion of the Kings the Republic assumed the task of protecting the oracles. Their care was given to men of the greatest distinction who are excused other public office or military service. They hold their position for life with public slaves as assistants. No-one else can consult the books. Indeed there is no other possession of the Romans, sacred or profane, which the Romans guard so carefully ... underground, in the temple of Capitoline Jupiter, in a stone chest guarded by ten men.

(DIONYSIUS OF HALICARNASSUS, *Roman Antiquities* 4.62.5)

The gods were definitely talkative when it came to Rome's last king. He received another omen soon after his purchase of the books. Two eagles made their nest in a palm tree in a garden near Tarquin's house. While the eagles were away hunting, a flock of vultures descended on the nest and killed the hatchlings. When the parent eagles returned the vultures attacked them as a group and drove the eagles from the tree. This was a sign that the reign of the Tarquin dynasty was coming to an end, just as an eagle had signalled the beginning by removing the hat of Tarquinius Priscus one hundred and five years previously.

VII

BIRTH OF A REPUBLIC

MISSION TO DELPHI

Yet another of the divine messages in Tarquin's omen-strewn life led him to seek advice, not from the Etruscans, but from the famous Oracle of Delphi in Greece.

> A fearsome portent manifested itself. A snake slithered from a wooden column, creating huge consternation in the palace. Tarquin himself was not so much terrified as deeply worried as to what this omen signified. For prodigies which affected the state as a whole he would generally use only Etruscan wise men. However he regarded this apparition as affecting him personally and so concerned was he that he decided to consult the most famous oracle in the world.
>
> (LIVY, *From the Founding of the City* 1.56.3–5)

Since this was a family matter, Tarquin's private embassy consisted of family members, so at this point a quick summary of the Tarquin family is needed. As is the case throughout Roman history the matter is complicated by the total lack of imagination in Roman nomenclature. It goes without saying that all daughters of the line were called Tarquinia in keeping with Roman naming conventions. The menfolk tended to be called Lucius, Sextus or Arruns. It comes as no surprise that three of Tarquin (Superbus)'s four children were Sextus, Arruns and Tarquinia with the fourth called Titus.

Meanwhile another Tarquinia – a daughter (or grand-daughter) of the first Tarquin, Lucius Tarquinius Priscus, had a son called Lucius, who was therefore the nephew of the current (Lucius) Tarquin on the throne. The father of this Lucius was Marcus Iunius, a descendant of the original band of Aeneas – and therefore someone with the aristocratic credentials to pose a threat to Tarquin's rule. This Lucius was an only child, because his brother and father had been executed by the suspicious Tarquin.

As the only surviving male member of the family, the younger Lucius got the message and removed himself as a dynastic threat by feigning mental incapacity. The Tarquins called him by the derogatory nickname 'Brutus', which means something like 'dullard', and adopted him into their household, all the better to keep a close eye on him.

Was Early Rome an 'Etruscan' City?

The reign of the Tarquin dynasty has led to the rather lazy comment that Rome in the later regal period was 'an Etruscan city'. This begs, to the point of abject supplication, the question of what is meant by the term 'Etruscan' city. Certainly the Etruscans had a huge influence on early Rome. Much of Roman art, architecture and religion came from Etruria, as did some basic concepts of writing and mathematics. And of course the Tarquins, rulers of Rome, were from an Etruscan city.

None of this is sufficient to define early Rome as Etruscan. Apart from the obvious differences in language and ethnicity, there is the basic fact that in the historical record (insofar as the record from those times can be called 'historical') Rome was part of Latium, not of Etruria. The city headed the Latin League, which would be a lot to ask of Etruscans. Etruria was not a political entity with a single government, so Rome could not have been Etruscan politically, and there is no indication that any other Etruscan city had hegemony over Rome. So to define Rome as 'Etruscan' we need to talk about culture.

However, if we are to call Roman culture 'Etruscan' we might go further and call the Etruscans 'Greek', since many of the ideas the Etruscans transmitted to Rome came from Greece (as did the Tarquins originally). In fact one ancient writer, Heraclides Ponticus, is quoted by Plutarch, who remarks that in his treatise 'On the Soul', Heraclides calls fifth-century Rome a 'Greek city' (*Life of Camillus* 22.2).

More properly it should be argued that Greece, Etruria and Rome all shared a Mediterranean-wide culture in which no single nation could claim to 'own' a particular idea. From religion to ship-building to pottery and architecture, ideas and techniques were part of a cultural melange deeply influenced by Egypt and Mesopotamia and spread by the assiduous efforts of Greek and Phoenician merchants, with everyone from Gauls to Hebrews to Scythians adding their contributions along the way.

Certainly the Romans picked up many ideas from their immediate neighbours, just as in later years the Romans absorbed so much directly from Greece that we refer to a Greco-Roman culture – but no one today claims that imperial Rome was a 'Greek city'.

This is also the moment to introduce another member of the family – the brother of Lucius Tarquinius (that is, Tarquinius Priscus, Tarquin the Elder, the late king). This brother was called Arruns (naturally) and died young, but not before he produced a son (another Arruns) who in turn produced a grandson of the line who was called Lucius. To distinguish him from the other Lucii Tarquinii this specimen is usually called Collatinus. Collatinus married an aristocratic woman called Lucretia. (The reason for this exposition will become clear later.)

Of this fine family group, Tarquin the king sent to Delphi two of his sons, Arruns and Titus, with Brutus tagging along for the ride. It is not known why Sextus, the other brother, did not come on the trip, but he may have been laid low by a plague which was affecting Rome at the time – indeed, Dionysius of Halicarnassus (*Roman Antiquities* 4.69.2) believed that finding a cure for this plague was the main reason for the mission to Delphi.

At Delphi the Tarquin brothers made pious offerings to Apollo, the patron god of the Oracle, and mocked Brutus who offered only a simple wooden staff. The Tarquin brothers did not know that Brutus had hollowed out the staff and inserted a rod of solid gold. They were somewhat startled, therefore, to find that their supposedly backward cousin was admitted along with them to their audience with the prophetess. What answer this seer gave to King Tarquin's original question is unknown, because it has been overshadowed in the literature by the importance of a second question, which one brother asked on the spur of the moment. 'Which of us shall next rule in Rome?'

The oracular reply was, 'He who shall next kiss his mother.'

The two brothers hastily made plans to get back to Rome before Sextus got affectionate with his parent, and barely noticed when Brutus, apparently overcome with excitement, confirmed his status as an idiot by stumbling and doing a face-plant into the earth. The 'idiot' had realized that Gaia, the earth, was the mother of all. In falling he had taken care to give the earth a smacking kiss, thus – in oracular terms at least – putting himself first in the line of succession.

The Delphic Oracle

Back at the dawn of time the god Apollo slew Python, a gigantic snake that had oracular powers (though these powers were apparently not good enough to see Apollo coming). This made Apollo the de facto guardian of Delphi, the site of the killing, and gave Apollo a secondary role as god of prophecy.

In historical times Apollo's Oracle was visited by thousands of people, from commoners looking for advice on domestic matters affairs to kings seeking guidance on matters of peace and war. Answers were given by a priestess of Apollo (the Pythia or Pythoness). It has been suggested that this woman was mildly intoxicated by natural ethylene fumes which seeped into her underground chamber.

Even the most sceptical of politicians might have been well advised to consult the Oracle. Delphi was at the centre of the world (the Greeks believed this to be literally true) and certainly its wide clientele of international visitors gave the priestess a uniquely well-informed view of world events.

Meanwhile back in Rome, Tarquin was preparing to go to war with the city of Ardea. This had less to do with any offence caused by that city and more to do with the fact that Tarquin wanted the rising discontent of his people to be directed at an external enemy. It helped that Ardea was rich and Tarquin needed money to fill the state coffers after his expensive public works.

By the time the Tarquin brothers returned from their trip to Greece war had begun. The Ardeans had refused to be rolled over by Rome's military might, and Tarquin had been forced to resort to the tried-and-trusted method of reducing the city by siege.

In this year (509 BC) the entire area controlled by Rome was some 50 kilometres (31 miles) across. Thus Ardea was close enough for someone with a good horse to put in a morning's fighting on the siege works and then ride home to sleep in his own bed at night. Even closer to Ardea was the city of Collatia, where lived that Lucius Tarquin who had the name of Collatinus. He and the other young Tarquins got into a dispute as to who had the better wife. Their homes being close enough for an impromptu visit, the party of young men visited each home in turn, where they found the wives socializing or relaxing. Only Lucretia, the wife of Collatinus, was hard at work weaving at the loom.

Smugly Collatinus invited the others to remain as guests for a while. This was a mistake, because Sextus Tarquin promptly fell in lust with his cousin's wife and became determined to have sex with her. A few days later he slipped unannounced out of the siege camp and made his way to Lucretia's house. There he threatened the unfortunate woman with a sword,

saying that if she would not lie with him he would kill her and a slave, lay the bodies together and claim that he had taken the pair in adultery.

Thus coerced, Lucretia submitted, but immediately on the departure of Sextus she summoned her father, Collatinus and Brutus. She revealed to them exactly what had happened, and made the men swear to make Sextus pay for his crime. Then she proclaimed, 'I acquit myself of the unchastity, but not of the penalty. No adulterer will in future excuse herself by pleading my example' (Livy, *From the Founding of the City* 1.58.10). With that, in front of her horrified family, she plunged a dagger into her own heart.

So perished the unfortunate Lucretia. Today it is hard to tell if the lady actually existed, but her story was to play a vital role in the rebellion that followed and that created Rome's Republic. Her violation and death gave the rebels a legitimate cause to rise against the royal family. At this time kingship was the norm and kings were naturally inclined to discourage those peoples who felt that the monarchy was dispensable. In order to justify an uprising against Tarquin the Proud, and in due course to prevent foreign powers piling in on Rome's new Republic, it was not enough to point out that the son of Tarquin had committed a rape. His victim had to be a perfect paragon of Roman womanhood.

Consequently, whatever the character of the real Lucretia (if she existed), any humanizing detail necessarily vanished as her biography mutated into a secular hagiography. The Lucretia of legend is modest, faithful, devout, hard-working, hospitable and strongly in favour of death before (or in her case, shortly after) dishonour. Given the patriarchal nature of the society which passed down these legends, we cannot now tell whether the Roman husbands' ideal of the perfect wife was shared by the wives themselves.

REBELLION

For Brutus the rape and suicide of Lucretia were the last straws. Taking the bloody dagger from Lucretia's fingers, he vowed by the woman's departed spirit that he would not live another day under the tyranny of Tarquin and his brood. He then passed the dagger to each of the others present, who swore the same oath. Collatinus was popular in the town which gave him his name and when the populace heard how his wife had been violated they barely hesitated before joining the incipient rebellion.

No one had expected Brutus the Dullard to take the lead, but once he had dropped his pretence he showed himself a capable and highly motivated leader. After a swift march on Rome he led into the Forum a mob consisting of armed citizens of Collatia and the city's militia. Once a crowd had gathered in the Forum, Brutus launched into a speech detailing the wrongs that Tarquin had done to the Roman people in general and his family in particular.

As it turned out, the Roman people were ripe for rebellion – all that had been lacking was someone to lead it. That leader they now found in Brutus, who quickly took control of the city. Tarquin was still with the army at Ardea. However, Tullia, his murderous wife, was forced to abandon the city in haste, spewing curses and threats of vengeance at everyone she encountered in her flight. While Livy seems to think that Tullia made it out of Rome in one piece, history and legend have no record of her thereafter. Perhaps few would have mourned if the Fates had, in fact, arranged for her to meet a violent end in a Roman alleyway, and thus perish as had her unfortunate father.

Appraised of the threat to his rule, Tarquin left the siege of Ardea and hurried to regain control of Rome, even as Brutus left in haste for Tarquin's camp at Ardea. The two men took different routes and bypassed one another unknowingly, so that each arrived at the point from which the other had started. They met with very different receptions. Brutus was received with joy as the army went over unconditionally to the rebel cause. Tarquin was met with closed gates, threats and a shower of insults. Rebuffed and now definitely an ex-king, Tarquin headed into exile in Etruria, already scheming how to regain his lost throne.

Sextus the rapist decided to return to the city of Gabii in the misguided belief that he could still rule there without the backing of his father and the Roman army. Consequently Brutus and his relatives were denied the personal vengeance which they had vowed beside the corpse of Lucretia. The people of Gabii had their own grudges to take out on Sextus and he was lynched on arrival.

Back in Rome Brutus quickly filled the power vacuum created by the absence of the king. He had himself and Collatinus elected as co-rulers and they took over most of the formerly royal functions. There was one major limitation on the power of the pair. They took office with the strict stipulation that they would serve for only one year. This, though the name and function of the office was to mutate considerably over the centuries, was the origin of the Roman consulship.

THE ROMAN REPUBLIC - YEAR 1

As might be expected after an abrupt coup and change of governmental systems, the reins of power did not pass smoothly into the hands of Brutus and his colleagues. Tarquin, like his predecessors, had been very much a hands-on monarch and there were numerous religious and constitutional functions which now needed someone to perform them. Several centuries later the Romans believed that they were still using some of the ad hoc solutions put in place by Brutus and his colleagues. For religious functions, for example, a sacred 'king' – the *rex sacrorum* – was appointed to take the royal role. This 'temporary' solution lasted until the Empire was Christianized in the late fourth century.

The Consular *Fasti*

In the ancient world one common method of counting the years was to go by the years of a royal reign. Actually this still happens, for in the Gregorian calendar now in common usage the current date is recorded as Anno Domini (AD) – that is, it counts the years which a medieval monk calculated as being the length of Christ's 'reign' on earth, starting from the supposed year of his birth. The more secular 'common era' versions of BCE and CE use the same date points.

Thus the first year of the Roman Republic was the twenty-fifth year of the reign of Tarquin the Proud. Thereafter the Romans counted their years by who had been consuls at the time. For example, the poet Martial remarks

'This Massic wine comes from the presses of Sinuessa.
Do you ask in whose Consulate it was bottled?'
(*Epigrams* 13.111)

Because the Roman consuls changed annually it
became harder to keep track of who was in charge when.
However, even in rebellion the Romans were a conservative
folk, and rather than change how they reckoned the years,
they simply started a list of consulships (*fasti*) and displayed
the result on stone tablets for consultation by the chrono-
logically challenged. This list was scrupulously maintained
throughout the history of the Republic.

Despite the vandalistic neglect by medieval popes of
their ancient heritage, the stone slabs have been preserved,
though not before papal builders had shattered them and
sold off much of the stone. Diligent scholarship was needed
to track down the fragments (the most recent was retrieved
only in the nineteenth century). Among those who worked to
piece the bits together in the early years was Michelangelo,
who is also on record as protesting against the use of the
Roman Forum as a quarry for building stone.

Because of their damaged condition the surviving *fasti*
start in the twenty-sixth year of the Republic, in 483 BC,
with consuls from the Fabian and Valerian families.

Tarquin still had supporters in Rome, for many aristocratic
families owed their status to his favours. Also Tarquin himself was actively criss-crossing Etruria and Latium to drum up
support for his restoration. He pointed out that allowing the
citizenry to depose their kings set a terrible example for local

monarchies, and also that the current political chaos in Rome provided the perfect opportunity for neighbouring states to quash that rising power.

VINDICATION

While a despicable character in many ways, Tarquin certainly lacked neither energy nor planning ability. As well as preparing threats from abroad, he had a plan for a counter-revolution at home. Firstly, Tarquin sent to Rome demanding the return of his personal property. While the Romans were debating whether to do this, the ambassadors set about achieving their real intentions – establishing which aristocrats were still loyal to the king and inciting them to rebellion.

The ambassadors found many among the aristocracy receptive to their message – even within the family of Brutus himself. This was not altogether surprising, for Brutus was himself a Tarquin by blood, and others in his family were less eager than he to relinquish the privileges of monarchy. Among those who joined the incipient conspiracy were the Vitellii, two of whom were senators, and also brothers-in-law of Brutus, whose wife was from the Vitellian clan. As the plot progressed, the sons of Brutus were roped in by their uncles. The traitorous group met at the house of the Vitellii to refine the details of their proposed counter-coup, unaware that one of the household slaves was listening and taking careful notes.

When the slave reported the plotters to the authorities a huge uproar resulted. The senate, which had been inclined to restore Tarquin's property to the deposed king, now reversed course and declared Tarquin's lands and goods forfeit as the property of a *hostis* (i.e. an enemy of Rome). Those accused

of conspiracy tried hard to deny the charges, alleging that the accusation had been brought by the slave out of personal animosity. The slave, however, had been careful to wait until he had seen the ambassadors and the plotters exchange written confirmation of their plans. These irrefutable proofs of guilt were discovered and the slave – who had been in considerable danger up to this point – was vindicated.

In fact, according to Livy, some of his Latin sources gave this event as the origin of the word 'vindicated', because the slave in question was named Vindicius. This leads modern readers to a chicken-or-egg situation, as it is at least equally probable that the name of the slave is a back-formation from the word *vindicatus*. That in turn takes its name from the *vindicta* – the staff which was formally touched to a manumitted slave's shoulder. After so many centuries we cannot now tell if the slave gets his name from the staff, or the staff from the slave.

In any case, the slave was freed and the conspirators sentenced to death – including the sons of Brutus. There was considerable speculation in the city whether Brutus would actually go through with the execution or if family loyalty would triumph over the demands of state. In fact Brutus made a treason trial unnecessary because he used his parental authority to execute his sons himself. (Roman law gave fathers the right to execute their offspring for any reason – or indeed for no reason at all – if the father was prepared to endure the social stigma for the terrible act.)

The execution of the sons of Brutus caused a problem for later tellers of the legend. This is because one of the most famous descendants of Brutus was that definitely historical Marcus Iunius Brutus who was among the murderers of Julius

Caesar. However, if the legendary Brutus had killed off his
children, and Tarquin had already killed the rest of the family,
where did his descendant come from? Also the first Brutus
must have been a patrician, since he was of the ruling class in
Rome, but the later Iunian clan were plebeians.

AFTER THE CONSPIRACY

The unravelling of the plot had several other consequences.
Firstly, there was a general revulsion not only against the return
of the king but against the Tarquin clan in general. Though he
had been an enthusiastic revolutionary, the fact remained that
Collatinus – who currently headed the government along with
Brutus – was actually called Lucius Tarquin, and the Roman
people were now adamantly opposed to having Tarquins of any
sort in government. In the end, when even Brutus advocated
his removal from office, Collatinus went into exile.

The second consequence is certainly legendary and demon-
strably false. The Roman senate, having declared the lands of
Tarquin forfeit, dedicated his fields to the god Mars – and
indeed the Campus Martius remained thereafter as a play-
ground, exercise area and training ground for Roman citizens
and soldiers for a millennium. However, at the time of the revolution these fields contained a bumper crop of grain, which
grain being now sacred to Mars, could not be used for mundane purposes such as making bread. In the end the Romans
dumped the lot into the Tiber.

This was in the autumn and the river was at a low point, so
instead of floating away downstream, the grain accumulated
on a mudbank and there trapped more and more debris until
a small island had formed in mid-river. Eventually the Romans

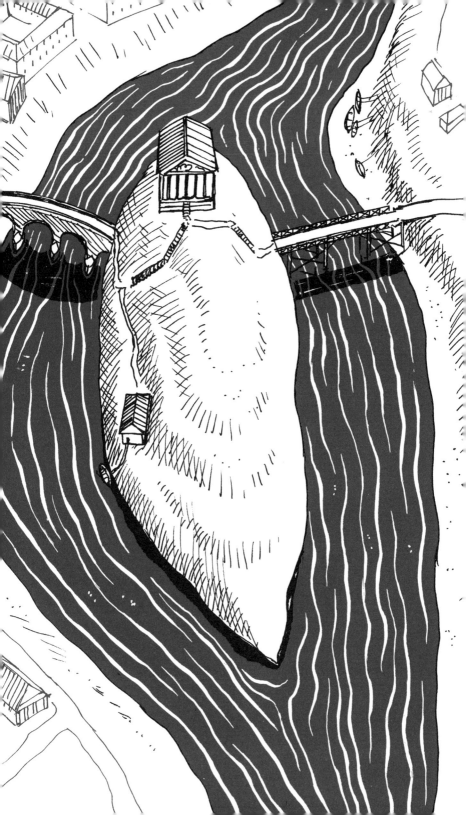

recognized the utility of that Tiber island and built it up further, later adorning the site with a temple to Aesculapius, the god of healing. Or so says the legend.

In reality, of course, the Tiber island is a rocky spur of the volcanic ridge which forms the Esquiline, Viminal and Quirinal hills to the east of Rome, and that outcrop has been there longer than the river itself.

The third consequence of the failed plot was that Tarquin decided to abandon subtle subversion in favour of an attempt to take Rome by brute force. He had persuaded Rome's inveterate foes from the city of Veii to join his cause, along with the army of the city of Tarchna (Tarquinia).

The opposing sides met in battle beside the Arsian forest (*silva*), after which (otherwise unknown) location this first battle of the Roman Republic was named. The battle of Silva Arsia began with a spectacular double knockout. Arruns, the son of Tarquin, was in charge of the Etruscan cavalry. Arruns recognized Brutus leading the Roman cavalry and launched an attack aimed at him personally. The cousins, Arruns and Brutus, were each focused on killing the other with no regard to personal safety, and both succeeded.

With Brutus and Arruns dead the cavalry of both sides was leaderless, and the battle devolved into an infantry slog which was finally won by the more motivated Romans. Valerius Poplicola, the surviving Roman general, led his troops back to Rome to celebrate the Republic's first triumph for victory in war.

To round off a very busy year, that September the Romans dedicated that temple to Jupiter on the Capitoline Hill, on the construction of which Tarquin had spent so much gold and political capital.

A TIME FOR HEROES

Tarquin was not yet done. He found a new ally in Lars Porsenna of Clusium and that king marched on Rome with his army. Livy claims that this was the chance for the Romans to show their stubborn spirit and embellish the city's traditions with some extra heroics. According to Tacitus (*Histories* 3.72), the Roman plebs rolled over and promptly surrendered.

Lars Porsenna

As king of Clusium, Lars Porsenna was one of the most powerful individuals in Etruria. (Note that he was not 'king' Lars Porsenna because 'Lars' is not a name but an Etruscan title which means roughly the same as 'king'.)

Although Tarquin was in the entourage of Porsenna, it appears that the Etruscan's motive in attacking Rome was not to restore the Roman monarchy but to take control of the city for himself. If the tales of heroic Roman resistance are indeed invention, it is clear that Porsenna's control of the city was not long-lasting. This is possibly because Porsenna soon afterwards became involved in an unsuccessful war with Aricia (the city from whence later came the mother of Augustus) and he found it expedient to repair relations with the Latins by withdrawing from Rome.

Pliny the Elder, writing in the imperial era of Rome, describes the tomb of Porsenna in Clusium. However, this structure was not extant in his day and the description of the edifice, apparently the bastard child of a pyramid crossed

HOW HORATIUS HELD THE BRIDGE

In the version of Roman history in which the city did not surrender, the Etruscan army came down on Rome like a wolf on the fold. Porsenna swiftly gained control of the Janiculan ridge on the west side of the Tiber. The Romans came out to meet the enemy in the field, and battle ensued. Things went badly for the Romans and they were forced into a rapid retreat that came close to being a rout. There was only one escape route for the retreating soldiery and that was over the only bridge which connected Rome with the west bank – the Sublician Bridge, which had been built by King Ancus Marcius over a century before.

The Romans were well aware of the risk from Etruria and had for that reason deliberately chosen to build the bridge entirely from wood 'without brass or iron', all the swifter to dismantle it should the Etruscans want to attack the city. However, they could hardly destroy a bridge full of retreating soldiery, and once the last Romans were across the first Etruscans would be too.

Step forward Publius Horatius Cocles, the junior officer who had been left in command of the bridge while the battle went on. This Horatius had a family tradition to maintain, as he was a descendant of that Horatius who had won the fight against the Curiatii two generations previously. (He was called Cocles, 'one-eyed', because he had lost an eye in a previous battle.) Horatius was joined in his defence of the bridge by two

Romans who had commanded the defeated army's right wing, Spurius Larcius and Titus Herminius.

These three held the bridge until the remnants of the Roman army had crossed. Then Horatius told the other two also to retreat, for their shields had been rendered useless by repeated blows. He also told the pair that the Romans should tear down the bridge behind him. In Dionysius's account (*Roman Antiquities* 5.24.2–3), he promised that he would personally ensure that no one got across in the meantime:

> After he had given the two men these instructions he made his stand on the bridge itself ... repulsing all who attempted to storm his position. Eventually the attackers stepped back. Being of the opinion that they were facing a lunatic berserker, no one wanted to come to close quarters. Nor was it that easy to get at him. He could not be attacked from the sides because of the river and in front of him was a pile of weapons and corpses. So they stood back and bombarded him with spears, javelins and rocks ...

> Finally he heard shouts behind him that the bridge was down ... whereupon he leapt into the river in full armour and made his way across the flow with great difficulty. ... He emerged on the riverbank without having lost any of his weapons in the crossing.

This, remarks Livy, was a feat more 'renowned than credible' (*From the Founding of the City* 2.10.11), and the historian Polybius, writing two centuries earlier, reckoned that Horatius leapt to a watery grave:

Cocles plunged into the river. Being as he was in full armour [and would therefore sink like a stone] he deliberately gave up his life. For him the safety of his country and the glory of his future reputation were more important than the years which would have remained of his life. Indeed I do believe that such legends inspire Roman youths [of today] to eagerly imitate such noble deeds.

(POLYBIUS, *The Histories* 6.55.3–4)

MUCIUS SCAEVOLA

Once the Romans had determined that the driving force in the war against them was not Tarquin but Lars Porsenna they determined to get rid of the threat by cutting off the head – that is, by assassinating the Etruscan leader. The assassin who came closest was a youth called Mucius, who successfully infiltrated the Etruscan camp. Unfortunately he picked as his target the man who was at the centre of activity in the royal tent. Consequently he stabbed what turned out to be the king's personal secretary.

The would-be regicide was promptly captured and introduced to the real king. Mucius defiantly informed Porsenna that he was merely the first in a line of would-be assassins. Other Romans sworn to kill the king were already on their way. Porsenna confessed to a natural curiosity as to the identity of these other killers and how they planned to do the deed. He threatened Mucius with torture unless the young man gave up the required information.

By way of reply Mucius shoved his hand into a nearby charcoal brazier and calmly watched it burn up in the hot coals. He explained, 'I came as an enemy to kill my enemy – and I am likewise prepared to die.' A somewhat bemused Porsenna ordered that Mucius be allowed to go free, remarking that the young man was in more danger from himself than from the Etruscans. Nevertheless, partly because he was impressed with the fanaticism of young Mucius and partly because the siege of Rome was taking longer than planned, Porsenna opened negotiations.

On his return to Rome, Mucius was hailed as a hero and compensated for his ruined hand with lands and a pension from the state. Since it would have impressed Porsenna just as much whichever hand he had burned off, it was something of an oversight on Mucius's part to have sacrificed his right. Thereafter he gained the cognomen – a cognomen being a sort of family nickname – of Scaevola, which means something like 'left-using' as he was thereafter forced to use this hand alone.

The Mucii Scaevolae endured as a family in Rome, though while Mucius was of the patrician class, his later descendants had, like the descendants of Brutus, somehow become plebeian. By then they had also changed the family's area of expertise. Instead of assassins, the Scaevolae of later Rome were better known for their expertise in the (some might say) less reputable profession of lawyers.

CLOELIA

Following the heroics of Scaevola, Rome and Lars Porsenna worked out a peace treaty by which Porsenna ceased his occupation of the Janiculan ridge in return for the Romans giving up lands they had seized from the rival city of Veii. Thereafter Lars Porsenna planned to set off immediately for Clusium, leaving behind his army's stock of foodstuffs as a goodwill gesture to the Romans. However, he intended to take with him a

number of hostages to make sure that the Romans kept their side of the bargain.

Among these hostages was an aristocratic woman called Cloelia. Her story is told by Valerius Maximus, a writer of the imperial period, in his book *Of Memorable Deeds and Sayings* (3.2.2):

> Cloelia almost sidetracks me from my main theme. Her daring deed happened at the same time [as the deeds of Horatius Cocles and Mucius Scaevola] against the same enemy alongside the same river Tiber. She and other maidens had been given as hostages to Porsenna. Yet in the night time she eluded her guards, stole a horse and on this hastened to the river and swam across ... A deed by a girl which acted as a torch of virtue for the men.

According to Livy (*From the Founding of the City* 2.13.8), Cloelia took a group of other female escapees with her, and they did not escape unobserved – in fact they crossed the river amid a shower of javelins.

Porsenna was impressed by Cloelia's bravery but pointed out to the Romans that this was totally inappropriate behaviour for a hostage. Unless the runaway was returned he would consider void the treaty by the terms of which the Romans had handed over the hostages in the first place. Yet when the Romans reluctantly handed back Cloelia, Porsenna did not punish her but instead praised her courage and allowed her to depart again with half the remaining hostages.

Romans of later ages commemorated the event by erecting a statue of Cloelia in the centre of Rome – the only known Roman statue of a woman on horseback.

VIII

OF PATRICIANS AND PLEBEIANS

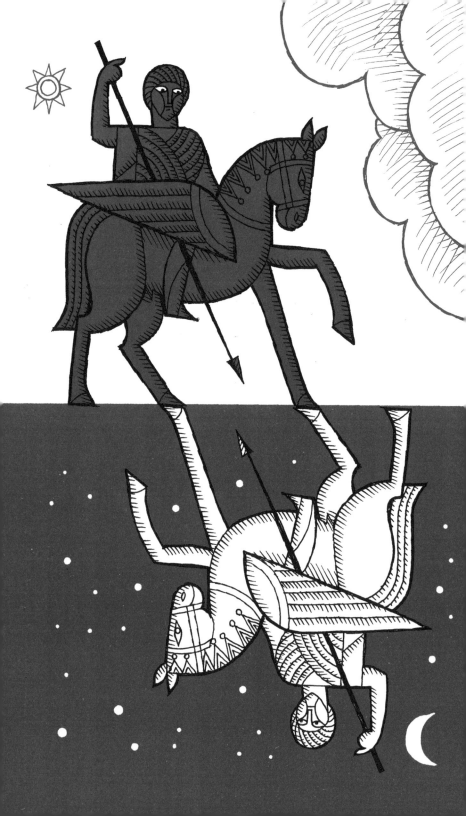

After 508 BC Rome was an established Republic. That did not mean that citizens enjoyed equal access under the law. In fact, most citizens did not even have any way of knowing what the law was. Roman law had yet to be properly codified, and it was left to individual magistrates to decide how cases should be adjudicated. These magistrates were invariably of the patrician class, and their judgments reflected this. This created a growing divide between the wealthy and powerful patricians and the poorer but more numerous plebeians. As a result the Roman state was torn by internal divisions at a time when external forces threatened its very existence.

One such threat was posed by ex-king Tarquin, who, despite having been exiled for over a decade, remained very much determined to regain his throne. Since the Etruscans appeared to have given up on his cause, Tarquin turned to the people of Latium. The Latins who lived outside the boundaries of Rome were understandably concerned about how long that condition would last. Rome remained an expansionist power, fighting regular wars and absorbing defeated enemies into itself. Tarquin took advantage of the Latins' fears. After Porsenna had ejected him from Clusium, Tarquin moved on to Tusculum where he married one of his daughters to the city's leader. Thereafter Tusculum became the leading state in the anti-Roman alliance.

The climax of the war was an epic and bloody battle fought at Lake Regillus some time around 495 BC. Herminius, who had held the bridge with Horatius, was killed in this action, as was the Tusculan leader. The Romans eventually prevailed, in part through the efforts of the cavalry – particularly two young cavalrymen whom the Romans later swore were none other than the mythical twins Castor and Pollux.

These two demigods, who today make up the constellation Gemini, were met before the battle by a member of Rome's Domitius clan (the clan that later produced the emperor Nero) as he watered his horses by a stream in the Forum. The pair assured Domitius that Rome would be victorious in the battle, and by way of proving their divinity, one of the young men touched Domitius on the beard – which promptly turned reddish-blond. Thereafter the clan were known as the Ahenobarbi ('bronze-beards'). At the site of the meeting a temple to Castor and Pollux was built – and indeed a temple remained at that location for the next thousand years. The remnants still stand today in the Roman Forum.

After his defeat Tarquin retired to the Greek city of Cumae in southern Italy where he died the following year. Rome made a treaty with the Latins by which their state was declared first among equals in the Latin League and all was well again – externally at least. Civic affairs in Rome were quite another matter.

A QUESTION OF DEBT

The dread of every ancient city-state was a condition that the Greeks called *stasis* – a sort of internal war, by which opposing factions might destroy their city through internecine rivalry. Livy tells how close Rome came to falling into this situation:

> The State was being ripped apart by internal conflict.
> The patricians and the plebeians were fiercely at odds ...
> The people complained bitterly that while fighting on the

battlefield for liberty and land they were oppressed and enslaved by their fellow-citizens at home, that war offered more security and peace, and they were safer among the enemy than with their fellow Romans. The popular anger was growing greater and more entrenched.

(*From the Founding of the City* 2.23.1–2)

Who Were the Patricians?

In modern terminology a 'patrician' is any distinguished and well-connected member of the establishment, though preferably one with a family history of similar record. As already mentioned, it may have been that the first patricians were members of a known family, rather than those new Romans who – wanted posters being also a feature in the ancient world – had hastily changed their names on arrival in the city.

Whatever their origins, Rome's patricians quickly developed into a separate, privileged class. At first the holding of public office and the major priesthoods were reserved for them. Patricians also married by a different rite to that of the common people, and certain types of clothing were reserved for them alone.

Over the centuries of the later Republic the plebeians managed to gain equal status with the patricians in most fields – though the patricians fought them tooth and nail most of the way. Even in the Late Republic the very patrician Julius Caesar was able to give public games in the role of *curule aedile* (magistrate elected from the patricians) – the more mundane task of administering the city infrastructure being left to the plebeian *aediles*.

One man, an ex-centurion who had won honours in battle, came to exemplify the plight of many Romans. While he had been away fighting in the Sabine war the enemy had pillaged his lands, driven off his livestock and burned down his farmhouse. Far from helping him, the Roman authorities had instead demanded money through an extra tax to finance the war, and in order to pay the tax the centurion had been forced to borrow at ruinous rates of interest. When he could not repay the debt he first lost his family land and then had to serve as a forced labourer in an underground workshop, with overseers who added whip marks to the scars he had incurred in battle.

It quickly became apparent that there were many others in a similar situation, and with that discovery the anger of the people boiled over. Rome was in turmoil and when news of this reached a neighbouring people called the Volsci, it was clear to them that this presented an excellent opportunity to attack the Roman state. Nor were the common people of Rome interested in fighting off the attackers since, as they pointed out, they would be leaving their lands unattended; and any loot from the war tended to go to the patricians who commanded the armies. Faced with an existential threat, the consuls promulgated an edict that no one could keep a citizen in debt-bondage when he was needed in the army and, while a man was serving, his property and family were safe from seizure by his creditors.

The Claudian Family

No family in Rome was as aristocratic as the *gens* Claudia, and few families had members who were so heartily detested by the Roman people. Legend tells that the founder of the line was a Sabine adventurer who made his fortune in a town called Regillum. Soon after the establishment of the Roman Republic, Attus Clausus, the patriarch of what was by then the leading family of Regillum, fell out with his fellow citizens (something Claudians were to do repeatedly in the centuries that followed). So unpopular was Clausus that he eventually sold off his property, packed the rest of his household into wagons and moved to Rome. There he Romanized his name to Appius Claudius and quickly became the leader of the most reactionary group in the Roman senate.

Attus Clausus was not the last of his clan to make the Roman people devoutly wish that the family had remained in Regillum. His grandson was every bit as unreasonable a would-be tyrant, who came close to starting a second revolution. Every generation thereafter at least one member of the Claudian clan could be found arousing either admiration for his service to the state or fury for his pig-headed defiance of the popular will.

Among the last members of the clan were the rabble-rousing demagogue Clodius – who mutated his name from Claudius to seem less aristocratic. Nevertheless the cachet of the Claudian name was such that the emperor Augustus married into the family to consolidate his reign, and the subsequent imperial dynasty is known today as the Julio-Claudian.

How much these measures were needed was shown by the fact that, though the Romans handily beat the Volsci, other neighbouring states took advantage of perceived Roman vulnerability to try their luck. The Romans had to fight several brief but savage campaigns before peace was restored – whereupon the senate promptly reneged on its promises to the Roman plebs.

With another war threatening with the Sabines, the consuls proceeded to call the levy. However, not a single man answered the summons. When the consuls tried to have their *lictores* (attendants) seize the defaulters the crowd pushed them back. At this point Appius Claudius led a faction in the senate that reckoned the people had reached this stage of mutiny because the consuls had not cracked down on them hard enough in the first place. 'Many thought the sentiments expressed by Appius Claudius were brutal and cruel (as indeed they were)', remarks Livy (*From the Founding of the City* 2.30.1), whose chronicle is our main source for these events. Finally, because no one trusted the consuls, the Romans – commoners and aristocrats alike – agreed to appoint a dictator.

Roman Dictators

In the ancient world a 'tyrant' was not necessarily a cruelly oppressive ruler but one who had taken power through unorthodox means – no matter how mild his rule thereafter. In the same way, a Roman dictator bore no relation to the preening fascists who are generally given that title in the modern era. For a start the Roman constitution decreed that a dictator could serve only for six months and be appointed only if the state faced a grave crisis of some description.

The Romans were keen supporters of the franchise, limited as it was, but they recognized that sometimes the give-and-take of a democracy acted as an impediment to swift and decisive action. Therefore, they allowed the consuls to nominate a dictator who thenceforth had precedence over other magistrates. However, those powers were intended to be directed only towards solving the crisis for which the dictator had been appointed and the dictator was accountable for his actions once peace had been restored.

After 202 BC no dictators were appointed until the perversions of the office under Sulla and Julius Caesar, both of whom appointed themselves as dictator after they had taken Rome by military force. One of the reasons for Caesar's assassination was that he became 'dictator for life' – though not for long.

THE SECESSION OF THE PLEBS

The newly appointed dictator came from the noble Valerian family. Valerius led the Romans to yet another triumph of arms. But yet again while the common soldiers were in the field, the aristocrats were working to undermine their cause at home. Even as the army paraded through Rome in triumph, creditors identified debtors among those in the ranks and pulled them away into servitude, something that so outraged Valerius that he resigned his office in protest. With the army in a state of near-mutiny the consuls hastily pretended that there was another military threat and tried to march the truculent soldiers out of the city. The army did march off – to a hill out-side Rome, where they called their families to join them. This is generally known as the First Secession of the Plebs. Another secession was to follow a generation later.

Rome became a city of patricians, which was rather a prob-lem for those with no experience of baking bread or cleaning out the latrines. On the other hand, the plebeians had plenty of experience at such activities and appeared capable of maintain-ing their secession indefinitely. Inevitably it was the patricians who blinked first. They sent their most skilled orator to see if he could bring the plebeians around with honeyed words (and, though Livy does not mention this, doubtless several meaning-ful concessions on the debt issue).

The orator, one Menenius, delivered the following famous speech – the Analogy of the Parts:

> There was once a time when all the parts of the human body did not work together as they do now. Every part had its own voice and opinions – and the general opinion was that it was unjust that all other parts had to work hard and concern themselves with getting everything for the belly. The belly meanwhile just sat in the middle doing nothing but enjoying the benefits which the other parts laboured to provide. So it was agreed that the hands would bring nothing to the mouth, the mouth would refuse whatever was placed within it, and the teeth would not chew it anyway.

> In this attempt to starve the belly into surrender the parts were subject to the same extreme debilitation that affected the rest of the body. This made it clear

that the belly was not simply sitting idly, but rather than benefiting from the work of the other parts it helped the body to live and thrive by distributing that nourishment it received by enriching the veins with the food it had digested.

(LIVY, From the Founding of the City 2.32.9–11)

Charming as this analogy was, it is more probable that the people were lured back to Rome by a more substantial promise. This was that the common people would be allowed magistrates of their own – and magistrates with very substantial powers at that. Firstly, as we have seen, the plebeians were allowed their own *aediles*. In later Rome these were responsible for the basic functioning of the city infrastructure though their role may originally have been limited to the maintenance of temples.

More important were the *tribuni*, tribunes, whose powers were so substantial that they could bring the state to a halt with their veto, arrest even a consul and protect any man from arrest. It is notable that when Rome came under the rule of the emperors one of the first powers Rome's new masters awarded to themselves was the tribunician power, which allowed them to do anything a tribune could do. Though these powers were largely limited to within the city of Rome itself, the protections offered by the tribunes were powerful indeed.

CORIOLANUS

The patricians were – to put it mildly – deeply resentful of having the tribunes foisted upon them, and the conservative faction in particular resented this check upon their power.

Among those who were most vociferous in their objections was a young aristocrat called Coriolanus (who had the first name of Gnaeus or Gaius depending whether one gives more credence to Livy or Shakespeare – though to be fair, Shakespeare has Dionysius of Halicarnassus in his corner. Plutarch, who wrote a short biography of Coriolanus, also opts for 'Gaius').

Coriolanus was of the Marcian clan. This was one of the oldest and most aristocratic families in Rome, which traced its line back through King Ancus Marcius to the city's second king, Numa Pompilius. In the second century BC a magistrate of this same family was to give Rome the enduring benefit of the Marcian aqueduct.

The cognomen (family nickname) by which this particular Marcius is best known came from the Volscian city of Corioli. So heroically had this Marcius fought in the conflict beneath this city's walls that he was given the name Coriolanus as an enduring mark of honour. (Corioli the town may be legendary, as may Coriolanus himself – the existence of both is seriously doubted by modern historians, and certainly there is no trace of Corioli in later annals.)

Coriolanus used his military distinction a few years later (the traditional date is 491 BC) when Rome was suffering from an acute shortage of grain. This had in part been brought about by the political shenanigans of the previous year, when the peasants who should have been sowing the fields had been roped into the army to deal with military emergencies and thereafter had spent their ploughing time sulking in the hills during the Secession of the Plebs.

To avert a famine, the senate had arranged for grain to be imported from Sicily. The question was now how to distribute this grain most fairly. Coriolanus had a different opinion of how it should be handed out. Forget fairness, he argued. Let the grain be given only to those who were prepared to reverse the concessions made after the Secession of the Plebs. Indeed, no grain should be distributed until the accursed institution of the tribunate was abolished altogether.

This was, in fact, exactly the sort of aristocratic abuse of power that the tribunate had been established to prevent, and the tribunes made this clear by charging Coriolanus with 'attempting to establish a tyranny'. Coriolanus disdained to answer the charges and his refusal even to appear in court led to a sentence of permanent banishment. Significantly, it appears that the senate had learned the lessons of the previous year and had no wish to refight a lost battle. They let Coriolanus know that he was on his own.

The extraordinary mobility of persons around the Mediterranean world has already been noted. Nevertheless, it was remarkable that Coriolanus sought refuge with the very people against whom he had distinguished himself by fighting – the Volsci. (Remarkable, but by no means unique – towards the end of the century the very historical Athenian general Alcibiades likewise sought refuge with the Spartans and was so accepted into Spartan society that he managed to impregnate the Spartan king's wife.)

Coriolanus returned to Rome at the head of a Volscian army which devastated plebeian lands but carefully spared those of Coriolanus's fellow patricians. Nevertheless, the plebeians, tired of war and desperate to get on with planting some crops, urged the senate to make peace. Coriolanus was adamant. First he refused to meet Rome's ambassadors, then he turned away a delegation of leading senators, and finally ignored a group composed of Roman priests. Negotiators, peer pressure and religion having failed, the senate was forced to turn to that power which no Italian lad could refuse – his mother.

That mother (whom Livy calls Veturia, but whom Shakespeare unaccountably calls Volumnia in his play) duly delivered the kind of harangue of which only an Italian matriarch is capable:

> How could you make me so miserable? What should
> have been the dearest sight of all – my own son, husband
> to this wife of yours [who had also been taken along]
> has been made horrible by seeing you at war with your
> native city.
>
> How can I even pray to the gods to alleviate my misery
> when I must ask either for victory for my people or safety
> for my son? What my enemies would call down as a
> curse, I needs must ask for should I pray. Your wife, your
> children, will either have to lose you or their homeland.
>
> As for me, I have to persuade you to find friendship
> and agreement where there is now division and enmity.
> Because otherwise I won't let war decide the issue.
> If you can't find a way to resolve things to everyone's
> benefit then know this – you are not going to attack
> your country without first walking over the corpse of
> the mother who gave you life.
>
> (PLUTARCH, *Life of Coriolanus* 35.2–3)

Given that ultimatum, Coriolanus had no choice but to retreat. By and large the Volsci were understanding. After all,

they had mothers of their own. However, the Volscian leaders had long been jealous of Coriolanus and, using his withdrawal as a pretext, they had him killed as a traitor to their cause.

With the Volscian threat removed, the grateful Roman senate ordered a temple built at the fourth milestone on the via Latina – the very spot where Veturia had confronted Coriolanus. The temple was dedicated to the goddess Fortuna, and more particularly to the goddess of good fortune for women (the Temple of Fortuna Muliebris). This temple certainly existed, for a stone has been found at the location with an inscription telling of the building's restoration by Livia the wife of Augustus. However, some sceptical modern historians believe that the legend of Coriolanus came into being to explain the existence of the then-ancient temple, rather than the temple coming into being through the existence of Coriolanus. (He is first mentioned in extant texts dating from some two centuries after his supposed death.)

LAND LAWS

For all its internal conflicts, Rome remained militarily successful. This was partly because the city was larger than most of its neighbours and thus was able to put more men in the field. Also most of the neighbouring states were autocracies of some description and autocrats have good reasons for not wanting the common people to get too much in the way of military experience. Being citizens of a republic, the Roman people felt that the state was exactly what the name says, a *res publica* or 'public thing'. It was their state, so they were all the more prepared to fight for it – and do so harder than those conscripted at the command of a king or tribal leader.

This meant that Rome had a habit of conquering the neighbouring peoples. When the Romans did not directly absorb the conquered people or cities into the Roman state, as the price for their forbearance they usually demanded a large chunk of the territory of the defeated people. This land became either public property – *ager publicus* – or was distributed to those who were felt to be deserving of it, possibly because they had paid the treasury a large amount of gold. Those with enough gold could also get use of public land by renting it from the state.

In fifth-century Rome people with that amount of money were almost invariably patricians and the common people began to get annoyed by the amount of land that patricians had managed to keep to themselves. This would have been all the more aggravating if hints in the ancient sources are correct and King Servius Tullius had actually passed laws limiting the amount of land that patricians could own. By renting land on the *ager publicus* the patricians were subverting the intent behind the laws.

Matters came to a head in 486 BC after another successful campaign had again increased the territory of Rome, this time at the expense of a people called the Hernici. It was suggested by a consul called Spurius Cassius that the land be distributed among the Roman plebs and the Latin allies who had helped Rome win this particular war.

Cassius had been consul during the Secession of the Plebs nine years previously and would have been well aware of the dangers of alienating the common people of Rome. Regrettably he proved less aware of the danger of alienating his fellow senators, several of whom had already taken possession of the more desirable Hernician properties. These senators spread rumours that Cassius was favouring the common people because he wanted their favour when he made an attempt to become king.

Matters were made worse when Cassius's fellow consul joined in the fray and launched a blistering attack upon his colleague. It is agreed that the unfortunate Cassius paid for his proposed legislation with his life. By some accounts he was hurled from the Tarpeian Rock, though other sources say that he was executed by his father, who employed that same power used by Brutus to execute his sons – namely that Roman fathers could legally kill their offspring for any reason.

Cassius is believed by some modern historians to be a semi-legendary figure, in that although he probably did exist (Cicero was clear that he had seen legislation dated with Cassius's consular year inscribed on a bronze tablet) his land legislation may have been a fictional back-projection of later struggles for agrarian reform in the second century BC. The Romans also felt that Cassius was considered a class traitor by the patricians, who kicked him out of the order. Later members of the family were therefore plebeian, including that later Cassius who gained some degree of revenge by leading the conspiracy which ended in sticking daggers into the highly patrician Julius Caesar.

The disputes between patrician and plebeian continued for centuries and were only finally resolved when the plebeians of Rome had become so integrated into the Roman aristocracy that it was impossible for anyone to pretend that they were anything but equal. Most patricians lived in the city of Rome itself (necessary if one were to regularly attend the senate) and Rome was so unhealthy that in antiquity the city has been described as a 'net consumer of people', which needed to be constantly refreshed by immigration.

As a result some great names of the Early Republic – the Horatii, Geganii and others – simply faded away. Others were elbowed aside by a new generation of plebeian aristocrats. By the time of Augustus, the patrician class as a whole was clearly dying out – not least because its members had been high-profile targets in the civil wars and proscriptions of the previous seventy-five years. Legislation was passed to create new patricians, but the title had really ceased to matter. The last known patrician of the families of old Rome, the magnificently named Servius Cornelius Dolabella Metilianus Pompeius Marcellus, died some time around AD 120.

THE IDEA
OF 'ROME'

This book has focused upon the legends of early Rome without paying close attention to whether the stories are factual or not. The key aspect – as Livy also points out (see pp. 6–7) – is that to a greater or lesser extent the Romans of later eras believed in these stories, and they shaped the people who became the Romans as we now think of them. But how much fact is there behind the stories?

While legends tend to suffer from exaggeration (who doesn't like an extra helping of handsome heroes and fickle gods?) they often retain an element of truth. It also helps the credibility of Roman legend that the storytellers usually hasten to propose a mundane alternative to divine or fantastic invention, such as substituting the apotheosis of Romulus with the senate murdering and butchering him instead. Divine interventions also tend to drop out of later parts of the Roman foundation story. There is not that much that involves the gods or that is intrinsically incredible about the account of the downfall of Tarquin (the histrionic suicide of Lucretia aside), nor in the political machinations behind the – possibly literal – fall of Spurius Cassius.

It is often pointed out that writers such as Livy described events that happened five hundred years previously. In fact

Livy himself points this out. The passage of that degree of time alone should not be enough to fuel incredulity – unless we want modern historians to believe that Henry VIII and his six wives or Sir Francis Drake and his defeat of the Spanish Armada are fantastical inventions. Or dispute the reality of Shakespeare, whose existence is about as well attested as the existence of Homer.

The passing of time is not the only factor which we must consider. Firstly, Elizabethan England, and Europe as a whole, was by and large a literate culture – or at least those who made history in the period were literate, and many of those records and even personal letters have survived. We do not know the level of literacy in early Rome (and are very uncertain of the level of literacy even in later Roman eras), but we do know that early Rome had largely an oral culture in which the tales of its founding and the regal period were passed down by word of mouth, probably for generations, before they were written down.

Oral tradition is enduring in its own way, because storytellers who deviate from a standard story tend to be corrected by their audience. On the other hand, audiences accept embellishment that reinforces ideas already present, so some Roman characters became archetypes. Numa was wise and a lawgiver, the man who established Rome's most ancient traditions, so any unexplained custom or religious rite could be attributed to him. Lucretia was not any victim but the flawless ideal of Roman womanhood, hard-working, virtuous and literally self-sacrificing. Roman menfolk in the legends are more like Achilles – far from perfect characters, but always unflinchingly brave and ferocious fighters.

Another reason for questioning the accuracy of Rome's early legends is related to one of the grimmest days in the history of the Republic. The day in question was, by the modern calendar, 18 July 390 BC, when the Romans took to the field to confront a force of Gallic invaders. Unused to the speed at which the Gauls manoeuvred their army, the ineptly commanded Roman levy was unable to properly deploy and was subsequently cut to pieces. Once its army had been wiped out, the city of Rome itself was defenceless, and the Gauls went on to sack it, killing most of the Roman senate in the process. The Romans fondly believed that a portion of their forces held out on the Capitoline hill. In this they were aided by geese from the Temple of Juno (to whom they were considered sacred) which warned of a Gallic sneak attack by night. Nevertheless, the rest of the city was occupied and comprehensively pillaged. As a result of the disaster most Roman records from the earliest days of the city were destroyed, leaving much of what remained of the history of that period as tales retained in the memory of the survivors.

There is considerable debate as to when the 'legends of Rome' become the 'history of Rome', and certainly the establishment of a written rather than oral culture does not prevent the creation of legend. Were this the case, the folk hero Johnny Appleseed would not exist in the United States nor the naked Lady Godiva in England. There remain many later Roman legends not related here, as this book is concerned with legends of the founding: first of the city and later of the Republic. These are the legends that told the Romans who they were and where they came from. Their legends told the Romans that their forebears were devout and brave. The women were chaste, bold and hard-working while the men were dedicated to the preservation and growth of the city. Lest a basic story of unrelenting virtue be too hard to swallow, there are plenty of exceptions that prove the rule and thereby make the tales of early Rome all the more intriguing and exciting.

Roman sensibilities were not modern sensibilities, and modern readers can find themselves appalled not only by some of the events described, but by the Roman treatment of them. The prime example of this is that crucial to early Roman history are three rapes: the rape of Rhea Silvia, which led to the birth of Romulus and Remus; the Rape of the Sabines, which established Rome for its posterity; and the rape of Lucretia, which sparked the fall of the Roman monarchy and the foundation of the Republic.

In narrative terms, none of these events had to have been precipitated by a sexual assault. Rhea Silvia could have been an ordinary princess rather than a Vestal Virgin, and Amulius would have tried to kill her children anyway. The Sabine women could have been bartered for in the manner traditional at the time. Given the level of hatred against Tarquin, a rebellion was inevitable. So the fact that legend does make rape the catalyst tells us something of how the Romans wanted posterity to view the founding of their city. It was not that contemporary Italian society didn't take rape seriously – it did (as demonstrated by the powerful reactions the three legendary instances provoked) and that fact was precisely the object of the stories.

The Romans regarded the foundation of their city as a transgressive act, defying the established order of the time. That's partly why the first generation of Romans includes a fratricide, mercenaries and, indeed, rapists. Cities were meant to be founded by respectable individuals, not a bunch of thuggish shepherds with no respect for convention. Even Rome's location was a disruptive act, disturbing trade flows and the local balance of power. Later came the establishment of a republic in a solidly monarchical region. Again, this was an affront to traditional mores. The legends insist that from the beginning Rome was different and outrageous, so key moments in its early history are likewise, and deliberately, shocking both to people of the time and (for different reasons) to us today.

We now see Rome as a sort of Borg-like entity which ruthlessly absorbed state after state until it had first taken over Italy and later much of the Mediterranean world. However the Romans did not see it that way. From their point of view, Rome started as a defiant but very vulnerable hilltop fort and the very nature of the founding meant that it was surrounded by unfriendly entities. All that the growth of the city had done was to attract a nastier class of enemy. So after being vulnerable to the Sabines and Latins in its early years, later Rome had to fight for survival against the Samnites, the Hellenistic army of Pyrrhus, the Carthaginians and invading Celts and Germans in the north. From the Roman perspective, the story of their city was not one of expansion and conquest but of holding out and thriving despite an unrelenting parade of ever more powerful foes.

Yet the legends of Rome also explain how the city survived. First of all, the Romans had the gods on their side with Jupiter, king of the gods, as their patron deity. From a modern perspective it seems strange that the often-immoral Romans enjoyed the support of the gods, but Roman gods were not particularly moral beings themselves. They regarded piety in terms of service to themselves rather than the toeing of an ethical line. From Aeneas (who is often described in verse as 'pious Aeneas') all the way through to the founders of the Republic, much is made of the devout nature of Rome's backstabbing, murderous but always god-fearing leaders. Even Tarquin the Proud had as his one redeeming feature his devotion to the gods, as evidenced in the building of the ruinously expensive Temple of Jupiter on the Capitoline.

Reassuring as it is to have the gods on one's side, in Roman legend the gods provide only moral, or at best indirect, support. Rome is not Troy, and the city's legends are not the *Iliad*. Seldom do Rome's gods take a direct hand in events as did Janus in the battle with the Sabines. Thus, rather than appearing as a vision to warn of attacking Celts, Juno lets her sacred geese do the work, just as it is a she-wolf and not a god who fishes Romulus and Remus out of the Tiber.

In fact, the Romans felt that their gods helped those who helped themselves. Divine beings might create the conditions for victory, but the Romans had to go out and win it. Which they did, thanks to their social cohesion and the sentiment later expressed by the poet Horace, writing under Augustus, of *dulce et decorum est pro patria mori* – that it is sweet and fitting to die for one's country. In short, there really was 'an idea of Rome', and that idea is explained in the stories that the Romans told themselves of how they, their city, and their empire came to be.

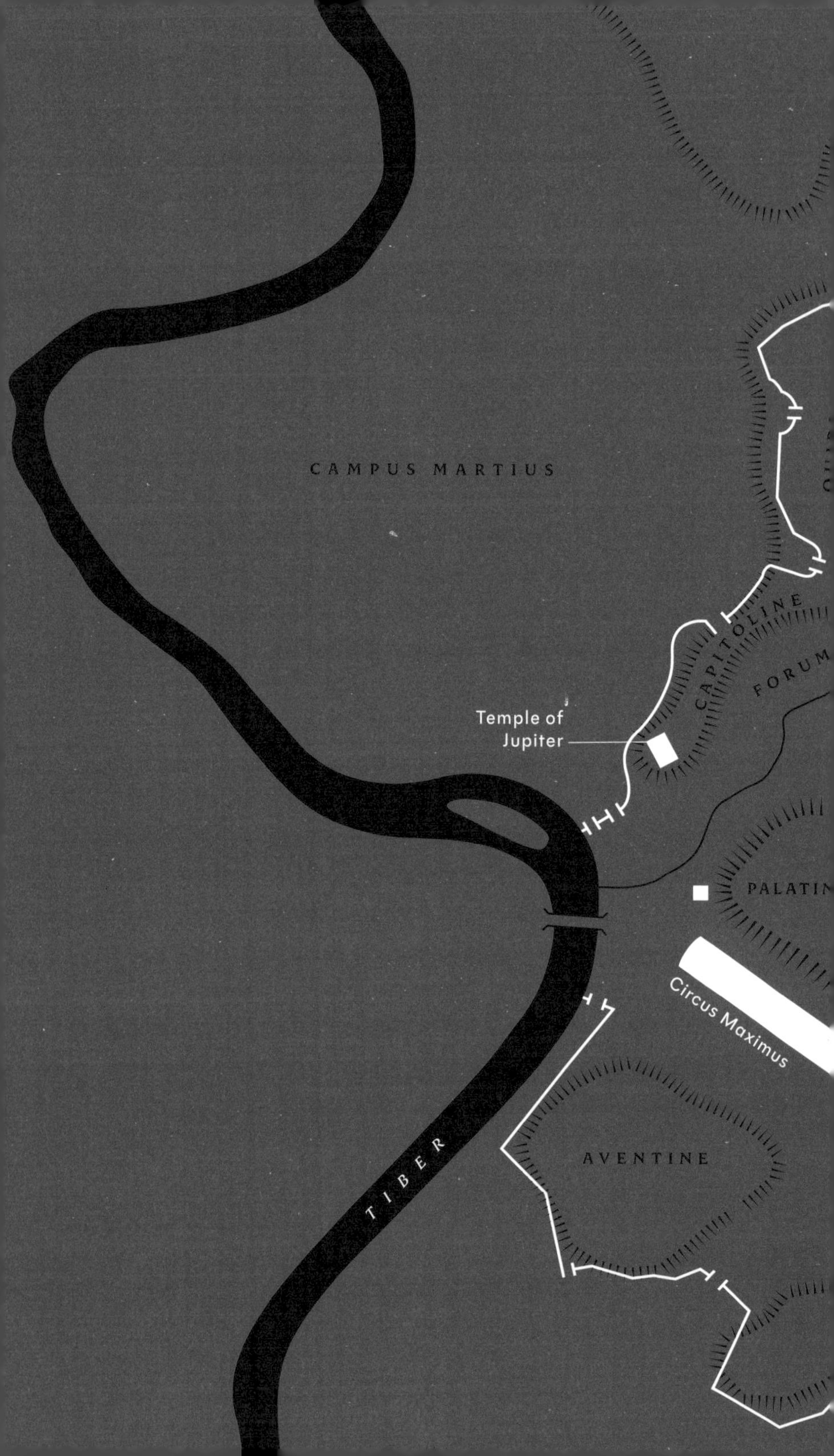

CAMPUS MARTIUS

Temple of
Jupiter

CAPITOLINE

FORUM

PALATIN

Circus Maximus

AVENTINE

TIBER

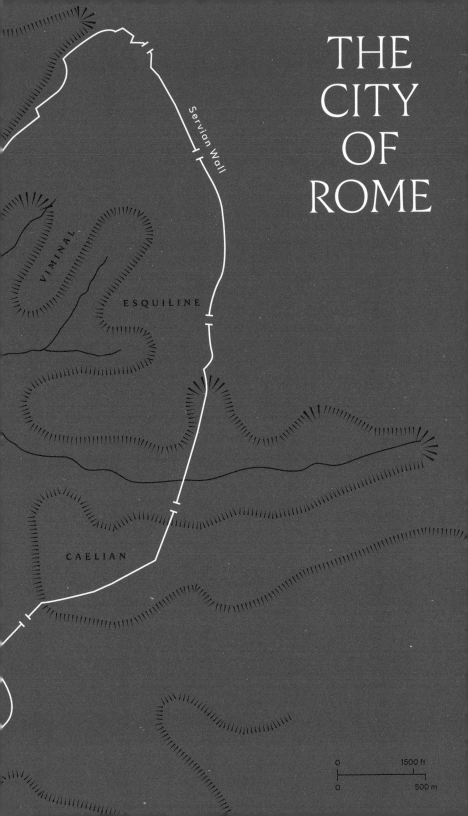

THE
CITY
OF
ROME

Servian Wall

VIMINAL

ESQUILINE

CAELIAN

0   1500 ft

0   500 m

DRAMATIS PERSONAE

THE ANCIENT WRITERS

Dionysius of Halicarnassus
55 BC–c. AD 10

Like Vergil and Ovid, Dionysius was a
product of Rome's Augustan age and
wrote some seven centuries after the
founding of the city. Famed in his day
as a teacher of rhetoric, Dionysius
is known today for a work usually
called *Roman Antiquities*. Used extensively by later writers – including
Plutarch – Dionysius was a careful
researcher who was prepared to admit
when he was drawing on folk tales
and legend.

Livy (Titus Livius) 59 BC–AD 17

Perhaps the most influential of all
historians of the Roman Republic,
Livy lived through the chaos of the
civil wars to the rule of Augustus,
who supported his work. Like
Dionysius of Halicarnassus he was a
careful historian who had access to
Roman archives for his work. Also
like Dionysius (and Plutarch) he was
no military man and relied on the
more competent reporting of his predecessor Polybius for his later writing
on the wars with Carthage.

Ovid (Publius Ovidius Naso)
43 BC–AD 18

Neither a historian nor biographer,
Ovid was a poet. For those interested
in the legends of early Rome, his
epic poem the *Fasti* is an invaluable
resource for the supposed origins of
many Roman traditions and religious
rituals. Regrettably the poet is not
bound by the historian's loyalty to
factual reporting, and his flights of
fancy often replace basic research. He
may not be the resource we want for
early Roman religion and anthropol-
ogy, but he is the resource we've got.

Plutarch c. AD 45– c. 120

We know a lot about ancient Rome
thanks to this priest and magistrate
who seldom left the little town of
Chaeronea in Greece, remarking
'I live in a small town and stay here
to stop it getting any smaller' (*Life of
Demosthenes* 2.2). A prolific writer, he
is known best today for his biogra-
phies (the *Lives*), which have enjoyed
such enduring popularity that in the
early years of the United States they
were outsold only by the Bible. His
Lives of Romulus and Brutus are almost
certainly fictional but tell us much
of what the Romans thought about
their founding fathers.

Polybius c. 200–c. 120 BC

Polybius originally came to Rome as a
hostage after the Roman conquest
of Greece. Unlike most of our
other sources he wrote during the
Republican period, but his work con-
centrates on the second and third
centuries BC. He does however
make tangential references to earlier
periods and is a valuable resource
when he does so.

Vergil (Publius Vergilius Maro)
70–19 BC
Another of our major sources for early
Roman history is a poet – in this case
perhaps Rome's greatest. Urged by
the emperor Augustus to compose a
poem on Rome's origins equal to the
Homeric classics, Vergil produced
a masterpiece drawn from existing
folklore and legends. His *Aeneid* tells
of the travels of the eponymous hero
from Troy to Italy several generations
before the founding of Rome. On
his deathbed, Vergil asked that this
work be destroyed; fortunately for
posterity, no one listened.

Others
While the above writers are our main
sources for early Roman legend,
they are complemented by a host
of others, including two whose works
are now lost but which certainly
informed the writers of the texts we
do have. These are Cato the Elder
who wrote his work *Origines* in Latin
perhaps in response to Rome's first
known historian Fabius Pictor, who
wrote in Greek. Pliny the Elder
provides many useful snippets in
his *Natural History*, and Cicero liked
to demonstrate his learned credentials by tossing in references to
Rome's early history. The first-cen-
tury AD historian Tacitus is very
reliable, but sadly (for our purposes)
he was interested almost exclusively
in events nearer his own time.

THE JULIAN FAMILY
(IN ORDER OF APPEARANCE)

Venus
The goddess known as Aphrodite to
the Greeks, she (allegedly) started
the Julian line by having a son with
the Trojan prince Anchises. Later
Julians, especially Augustus and
Julius Caesar, made much of their
divine origins.

Anchises
Father of Aeneas, he was already aged
when the Greek sack forced him to
flee from Troy.

Aeneas
The man who brought the Trojan
refugees to Italy and merged them
with the Latin people. He abandoned
Queen Dido of Carthage to fulfil
his destiny, giving rise to numerous
dramas and operas and (according to
Vergil) the later Punic Wars.

Iulus (aka Euryleon/Ascanius)
The polyonomous son of Aeneas who
founded the city of Alba Longa, the
birthplace of Romulus and Remus.
Namesake of the Julian line.

Silvius
King of Alba Longa and founder of
the Silvian line. Due to dynastic dif-
ficulties he spent his early years
hiding out in the forest (*silva* in
Latin) – hence the family name.

Tiberinus
An Alban king who drowned in
the river which was subsequently
named after him.

Aventinus

The great-great grandfather of Romulus and Remus, buried on one of the seven hills of Rome that was thereafter called the Aventine.

Numitor

Grandfather of Romulus and Remus. Cheated of the Alban throne by his dastardly brother Amulius but restored by the twins.

Amulius

Dastardly brother of Numitor. Came to a sticky end when he was overthrown by Romulus and Remus for mistreating their mother and throwing them into the Tiber.

Rhea Silvia

Daughter of Numitor and mother of Romulus and Remus after violation by either the god Mars or Amulius. Depending on your choice of legend, she was either executed by Amulius or happily reunited with her sons.

Romulus and Remus

The founders of Rome. Remus was killed by a follower of his brother during a fraternal argument, and Romulus was either apotheosized as the god Quirinus or chopped to pieces by unfriendly senators (again, depending on your choice of legend).

Proculus Julius

Promoter of the theory that Romulus became a god. Mainly notable for marking the reappearance of the Julian line in the 'historical' record.

Augustus Caesar

Proud heir of the noble Julian line and descendant of Venus. Restorer of Rome after the civil wars and an expert propagandist who made sure that the writers and poets of his day made his alleged origins perfectly clear.

ROMAN KINGS AND CONSULS

Titus Tatius

Sabine king and later co-ruler of Rome with Romulus under the peace terms agreed after the abduction of the Sabine women. His undiplomatic handling of the neighbours led to his lynching by an indignant mob.

Numa Pompilius

According to legend, Numa was the source of every ancient religious rite and every venerable tradition. Also a Sabine, he gave Rome relief from the wars that the city continually conducted before (and after) his reign.

Tullus Hostilius

Warrior king who conquered Alba Longa and removed the population to Rome. He died after bungling a sacrifice to Jupiter and was smitten by a thunderbolt.

Ancus Marcius

Grandson of Numa, he extended Rome's territory and formalized some rituals established by Numa.

Lucius Tarquinius Priscus
(Tarquin the Elder)

From a family exiled from Corinth, Tarquin took his name from the

Etruscan town of Tarquinia where he lived before moving to Rome. Assassinated by the jealous sons of Ancus Marcius.

Servius Tullius
Originally brought to Rome as a captive. After various divine manifestations showed he was to be the city's next ruler, he was adopted as son and heir by Tarquinius. Despite being good at the job, Rome's aristocracy saw Servius as a usurper. Alleged builder of Rome's 'Servian' walls.

Lucius Tarquinius Superbus (Tarquin the Proud)
Competent, but arrogant, with a habit of executing those he disliked. His major achievements were building a temple to Jupiter on the Capitoline hill and a sewer under the Forum. The temple lasted for the next thousand years, and the sewer is still operational. Finally overthrown by the Roman aristocracy.

Lucius Iunius Brutus
Liberated Rome from Tarquin's rule. After years avoiding execution by the suspicious king (to whom he was related), he led Rome's uprising and died in the wars that followed. Executed his own sons for conspiring with the deposed Tarquin.

Attus Clausus (Appius Claudius)
Founder of Rome's great Claudian family which produced two emperors and numerous consuls and other magistrates.

Spurius Cassius
Three times consul, his standing with the people made the aristocracy fear he was plotting to become king so he was executed.

OTHER KINGS

Picus
A legendary king in the area that was to become Rome. He was turned into a woodpecker for rejecting the sorceress Circe (which is why today woodpeckers are in the genus *Picus*).

Evander
Greek king of Pallantium, the pre-Roman settlement on the seven hills.

Priam
King of Troy and relative of Aeneas. Killed by the son of Achilles when the city was taken by the Greeks.

Latinus
The local king in the area where the Trojan Aeneas landed. His daughter Lavinia married Aeneas to create the progenitors of the Roman people.

Lars Porsenna
Etruscan king (which is what 'Lars' translates to) of Clusium. An honourable opponent who supported Tarquin the Proud's restoration with his army.

NOTABLE WOMEN

Roma

By one tradition a woman who, sick of being a peripatetic refugee, burned the Trojans' boats when they were moored along the Tiber. Discovering they were marooned in a good location, the Trojans named the city they founded there after her.

Dido of Carthage

A refugee from Tyre who founded Carthage. Before Vergil decided to explain the Punic Wars by having Aeneas abandon Dido and create eternal enmity between Romans and Carthaginians, Dido died to prevent a local king from taking control of her city.

Larentia

Wife of the shepherd Faustulus who found Romulus and Remus as abandoned babies. One tradition says she was a prostitute or *lupa*, which is also the Latin for 'she-wolf'.

Hersilia

The wife of Romulus. Abducted along with the other Sabine women, she became a paid-up subscriber to the Roman project and was key in mediating peace between the Sabines and Romans.

Tarpeia

A Vestal Virgin who conspired to betray Rome by allowing the Sabines to attack the Capitoline hill. Although they benefited from it, the Sabines killed her for her treachery.

Egeria

A nymph who canoodled with king Numa and allegedly helped him with sorting out the government of Rome's unruly population.

Horatia

A Roman woman pledged to marry one of the Alban Curiatii. She was understandably absent when her brother killed the man in the Battle of the Champions. The brother (also highly emotional because the Curiatii had just slain two of his brothers) took exception to her grief and killed her on the spot.

Tanaquil

Wife of Tarquinius Priscus and originally from an aristocratic Etruscan family. She encouraged her husband to move to Rome where his prospects were better.

Tullia

Wife of Tarquin the Proud. As ambitious and murderous as her spouse she supported his coup against her father and callously drove over her father's corpse in her chariot.

Lucretia

Seen by later generations as an idealized Roman matron. She committed suicide after being raped by a relative of Tarquin the Proud and thus sparked the revolution that led to the creation of the Roman Republic.

Cloelia

A Roman hostage who helped other hostages escape from Lars Porsenna. This violated the prevailing ceasefire, but the Romans admired her indomitable spirit.

Veturia

The mother of the Roman aristocrat Coriolanus. Coriolanus went rogue and allied with Rome's enemies until Veturia stopped his march on the city with a good telling-off.

FRIENDS, ROMANS AND OTHERS

Cacus

A legendary and infamous bandit who terrorized the countryside around the seven hills that later became Rome. The temple allegedly created to celebrate his death at the hands of Hercules still stands in modern Rome.

Mettius Curtius

A Sabine aristocrat who got bogged down in the Roman Forum (which was then a marsh). The location where this happened became known as the Lacus Curtius. A later member of the family allegedly threw himself into a crevice which opened at the site, and by his self-sacrifice saved Rome.

Collatinus (aka Lucius Tarquin)

Husband of Lucretia. Despite being a leading revolutionary in the creation of the Republic he was forced into exile by Brutus because of his kinship with the Tarquin family.

Arruns, Lucius, Sextus, Titus

Personal names of the Tarquins. Because the family stuck exclusively to these names even contemporary Romans got somewhat confused about who was who.

Vindicius

A slave who revealed details of an aristocratic plot to betray the Republic to Tarquin. It was alleged that he made the denunciation through malice, but after the discovery of incriminating documents he was vindicated.

Horatius Cocles

Another noble member of the ancient Horatii family he is mainly famous for holding the bridge (the Sublician Bridge to be precise) against the Etruscan army of Lars Porsenna.

Herminius

A Roman who fought alongside Horatius in holding the bridge. Later made consul for his efforts he died in the Battle of Lake Regillus, where Roman victory secured the city's dominance in Latium.

Mucius Scaevola

A Roman who attempted to assassinate Lars Porsenna. To prove his contempt for torture he voluntarily thrust his hand into a burning brazier, an act of fanaticism that made Lars Porsenna decide to make peace.

Valerius Poplicola

One of the first Roman consuls, he attempted to mediate in the social struggles of the Early Republic (the 'Conflict of the Orders')

GLOSSARY OF LATIN TERMS USED IN THE TEXT

ager publicus 198
Lands owned by the Roman state.

augurium (augury) 127, 144
A sign from the gods sent to a
designated watcher (augur).

auspicium (auspices) 64, 89
The outcome of the signs sent
by the gods.

carpentum 124
A type of carriage.

cognomen 178, 193
In Roman names, an identifier for an
individual or family branch.

collegium 112
A professional body, e.g. of magistrates
or priests.

concilium 100
A consultative meeting of any kind.

fasti 165–66
Lists of seasons, festivals and
magistrates.

gens 11, 90, 187
Rather like a clan.

gentilicium 111
The main family identifier in Roman
names, e.g. Gaius Julius Caesar
indicates he is of the Julian family
(*gens* Iulia).

hostis 68, 167
An enemy of the state.

mores 206
Traditionally accepted conduct.

patres 96
Heads of families.

pomerium 67–8
The sacred boundary of Rome.

porta 68, 139
A city gate.

prodigium (prodigy) 148, 154
A sign from the gods that something
is afoot.

proscriptio (proscription) 200
A purge of 'enemies' of the state.

raptus 77
Captured violently.

res publica 197
The 'public thing' – the Roman
Republic.

sibyl 150
A female soothsayer.

spina 73
The dividing barrier on a chariot
racetrack.

stasis 184
Civil strife, close to civil war.

tullius 121
A spring of water.

ver sacrum 40
Sacred Spring.

vindicta 169
A staff used to formally manumit
a slave.

FURTHER
READING

Beyer, B., *Legends of Early Rome* (New Haven and London: Yale University Press, 2015)

Read the legends in the original Latin arranged for beginners. Pair with Neel, 2017 (see below).

Carandini, A., *Rome: Day One*, trans. S. Sartarelli (Princeton: Princeton University Press, 2011)

Archaeology in support of legend. A controversial book but an intriguing read.

Cornell, T., *The Beginnings of Rome* (London: Routledge, 1995)

Forsythe, G., *A Critical History of Early Rome from Prehistory to the First Punic War* (Berkeley: University of California Press, 2005)

This can be read as a counter to Cornell, who Forsythe feels takes the sources too literally.

Fraccaro, P., 'The History of Rome in the Regal Period', *Journal of Roman Studies*, 47/1–2 (November 1957), 59–65, published online by Cambridge University Press, 2012

A heavyweight tome in all senses of the word.

Livy, *The Early History of Rome: Books I–V*, trans. A. de Sélincourt (London: Penguin Classics, 2002)

The definitive source.

Neel, J. (ed.), *Early Rome: Myth and Society*, Blackwell Sourcebooks in Ancient History (Hoboken: Wiley-Blackwell, 2017)

The original texts in translation.

Serres, M., *Rome: The First Book of Foundations*, trans. R. Burks (London: Bloomsbury, 2015)

Philosophical musings on themes connected with the legends.

INDEX

PHILIP MATYSZAK has a doctorate in Roman history from St John's College, Oxford. He also teaches and prepares courses for the eLearning programme at Cambridge University. He is the author of numerous books on the ancient world, including *Lost Cities of the Ancient World* (2023), *The Greek and Roman Myths* (2010) and *Ancient Magic* (2019), all published by Thames & Hudson.

First published in the United Kingdom in 2025 by
Thames & Hudson Ltd, 181A High Holborn, London WC1V 7QX

First published in the United States of America in 2025 by
Thames & Hudson Inc., 500 Fifth Avenue, New York, New York 10110

Rome Before Rome © 2025 Thames & Hudson Ltd, London

Text © 2025 Philip Matyszak
Illustrations by Joe McLaren

British Library Cataloguing-in-Publication Data
A catalogue record for this book is available from the British Library

Library of Congress Control Number 2024946128

ISBN 978-0-500-02831-5

Impression 01

Printed and bound in China by Shenzhen Reliance Printing Co. Ltd

Be the first to know about our new releases,
exclusive content and author events by visiting
thamesandhudson.com
thamesandhudsonusa.com
thamesandhudson.com.au